Proving
the Value
of HR

Practical HR Series

Proving the Value of HR

How and Why to Measure ROI

Jack J. Phillips and
Patricia Pulliam Phillips
Society for Human Resource Management
Alexandria, Virginia
USA
www.shrm.org

This publication is designed to provide accurate and authoritative information regarding the subject matter covered. It is sold with the understanding that neither the publisher nor the author is engaged in rendering legal or other professional service. If legal advice or other expert assistance is required, the services of a competent, licensed professional should be sought. The federal and state laws discussed in this book are subject to frequent revision and interpretation by amendments or judicial revisions that may significantly affect employer or employee rights and obligations. Readers are encouraged to seek legal counsel regarding specific policies and practices in their organizations.

This book is published by the Society for Human Resource Management (SHRM®). The interpretations, conclusions, and recommendations in this book are those of the author and do not necessarily represent those of SHRM.

The Society for Human Resource Management (SHRM) is the world's largest professional association devoted to human resource management. Our mission is to serve the needs of HR professionals by providing the most current and comprehensive resources, and to advance the profession by promoting HR's essential, strategic role. Founded in 1948, SHRM represents more than 225,000 individual members in over 125 countries, and has a network of more than 575 affiliated chapters in the United States, as well as offices in China and India. Visit SHRM at **www.shrm.org**

HR: Leading People, Leading Organizations

Edited by: Karen Eddleman
Index by: Sharon Johnson
Cover design by: Carol Williams
Interior design by: Shirley Raybuck

Library of Congress Cataloguing-in-Publication Data
Phillips, Jack J., 1945-
  Proving the value of HR : how and why to measure ROI / Jack J. Phillips and Patricia Pulliam Phillips.
    p. cm. — (Practical HR series)
  Includes bibliographical references and index.
  ISBN 978-1-586440-49-7
  1. Personnel management. 2. Rate of return. I. Phillips, Patricia Pulliam. II. Title. III. Series.

HF5549.P4595 2005
658.3'125—dc22

                                2004028403

Printed in the United States of America.
10 9 8 7 6 5 4 3

Contents

i

Illustrations

Figures

Tables

CD-ROM Contents

Section 1: Assessment and Current Status
CD-ROM Figure 1a HR Self-Test
CD-ROM Figure 1b HR Self-Test: Scoring and Interpretation
CD-ROM Figure 1c HR Self-Test: Analysis
CD-ROM Figure 2 Paradigm Shift Exercise
CD-ROM Figure 3 HR Contribution: Exercise

Section 2: Planning
CD-ROM Figure 4 Evaluation Planning: Worksheet
CD-ROM Figure 5a Wachovia Bank Case Study:
      Isolation & Conversion Questions
CD-ROM Figure 5b Wachovia Bank Case Study: Discussion of Answers
CD-ROM Figure 6 Data Collection Plan
CD-ROM Figure 7 ROI Analysis Plan

Section 3: Setting Objectives
CD-ROM Figure 8a Department of Internal Affairs Case Study:
      Levels of Evaluation Questions
CD-ROM Figure 8b Department of Internal Affairs Case Study:
      Discussion of Answers
CD-ROM Figure 9a Matching Evaluation Levels to Objectives: Exercise
CD-ROM Figure 9b Matching Evaluation Levels to Objectives: Answer Key
CD-ROM Figure 10 Developing Reaction and Satisfaction Objectives
CD-ROM Figure 11 Developing Learning Objectives
CD-ROM Figure 12 Developing Application Objectives
CD-ROM Figure 13 Developing Business Impact Objectives

Section 4: Data Collection

Section 5: Isolating the Effect of the HR Program

Section 6: Converting Data to Monetary Values

Section 7: HR Program Costs

Formulas

References

Acknowledgments and Attributions

Resources from the Authors

Preface

Though your balance-sheet's a model of what a balance-sheet should be,
Typed and ruled with great precision in a type that all can see;
Though the grouping of the assets is commendable and clear,
And the details which are given more than usually appear;
Though investments have been valued at the sale price of the day,
And the auditor's certificate shows everything O.K.;
One asset is omitted—and its worth I want to know,
The asset is the value of the men who run the show.

(Archibald Bowman, "Reporting on the Corporate Investment,"
Journal of Accountancy, May 1938, p. 399)

For decades, organizations have struggled with placing a value on employees and, more specifically, on the value of human resources (HR) programs.

Today's HR professionals need a balanced set of measures and processes to show the value of the HR contribution. Measuring the return on investment (ROI) is emerging as a promising tool to provide convincing data about the contribution of specific HR programs and processes. It is now a part of the measurement mix.

The interest in ROI has been phenomenal. The topic appears on almost every human resources development (HRD) conference and convention agenda. Articles on ROI appear regularly in HRD practitioner and research journals. Several related books have been published on the topic, and consulting firms have sprung up overnight to tackle this critical and important issue.

Several issues are driving this increased interest in ROI and its application to a variety of HR programs. Pressure from clients and senior managers to show the return on their HR investment is probably the most influential driver. Competitive economic pressures are causing intense scrutiny of all expenditures, including all training and development costs. Total quality management, re-engineering, and continuous process improvement have renewed interest in measurement and evaluation, including measurement of the effectiveness of HR. The general trend toward accountability with all staff support groups is causing some HRD departments to measure their contribution. A few progressive HR departments have taken a proactive approach; without any prodding or encouragement from above, they are using ROI to measure their contribution. In all, these and other factors have generated an unprecedented wave of applications of the ROI process.

Return on investment has become one of the most challenging and intriguing issues facing the HR field. The challenging aspect of the process is the nature and accuracy of its development. The process often seems confusing, surrounded by models, formulas, and statistics that often frighten the most capable practitioners. Many in the HR field got into it initially because they loved working with people, not numbers. Coupled with this concern are misunderstandings about the process and the gross misuse of ROI techniques in some organizations. These issues sometimes leave practitioners with distaste for the process. Unfortunately, ROI cannot be ignored. To admit to clients and senior managers that the impact of HR cannot be measured is to admit that HR programs do not add value or that the HR department should not be held accountable for its impact—positive or negative—on the organization's bottom line. In practice, ROI must be explored, considered, and ultimately implemented in almost every organization—whether it is for profit or nonprofit, public or private.

What is needed is a rational, logical approach that can be simplified and implemented within the constraints imposed by the organization's budget and resource availability. This book presents a proven ROI process based on almost 20 years of development and refinement. It is a process that is rich in tradition but sophisticated enough to meet the demands facing training and performance improvement programs.

Why This Book? Why Now?

When examining current publications related to ROI, we discovered there is no book with a practical, concise presentation on ROI for HR.

Most representations of the ROI process ignore or provide little insight into the two key elements essential to developing the ROI: isolating the effects of training and converting data to monetary values. Recognizing that many other factors influence output results, this book provides several strategies to isolate the effects of HR—far more than any other presentation on the topic. Scant attention has been given to the issue of assigning monetary values to the benefits derived from HR programs. This book presents key strategies for converting data to monetary values.

This book was developed at the request of many clients and colleagues who asked for a simplified, concise description of the ROI methodology, presented in a step-by-step approach. Our earlier contributions to the ROI process include two successful books, *The Human Resources Scorecard: Measuring Return on Investment* (with Ron D. Stone, 2001, Butterworth-Heinemann) and *Return on Investment in Training and Performance Improvement Programs*, second edition (2003, Butterworth-Heinemann).

What is needed, according to practitioners, is a book that addresses the ROI process for HR and presents an approach that is rational, feasible, and understandable to the typical HR practitioner. We designed this book to meet this need.

Who Can Benefit from This Book?

HR professionals in both private and public organizations are the primary audience for this book. With its step-by-step approach and case applications, it is also be useful as a self-study guide for this important group. Whether an individual is involved in HR consulting, design, implementation, coordination, or evaluation, this book is an indispensable reference. Individuals in all functional aspects of HRD should find the book valuable. These include recruiting and selection, education and learning, compensation and benefits, employee relations, compliance and fair employment practices, human capital management systems, and HR consulting services. The ROI process described in the book has been used to measure a variety of HR programs. Individuals in HR leadership positions (managers, supervisors, team leaders, directors, vice presidents) will find this book to be a valuable addition to their professional library.

Another audience is the management group. Because of the tremendous interest in ROI among the management team and clients, this book should be a useful reference for them. In a simple, easy-to-implement process, it shows how the ROI is developed in language that managers, administrators, and executives understand.

Consultants, professionals, researchers, and seminar presenters will find the ROI methodology to be an effective way to measure the impact of HR programs. The book provides a workable model for consultants to evaluate change initiatives or consulting interventions. The book provides researchers with a sound tool for evaluating a variety of HR programs. Its content should stimulate thought and debate about how the ROI is developed and applied. Finally, the book should be a useful textbook or supplemental book for a course on HR evaluation.

How Is This Book Organized?

This book presents the ROI model in a step-by-step process. Typically, a chapter is devoted to each major part of the model as the pieces of the ROI puzzle are methodically assembled. At the conclusion, the reader has a clear understanding of the overall ROI process.

Chapter 1, "The Accountability Crisis," explains the issues and concerns about the HR contribution as it traces the key influences for increased accountability. The payoff of increased investment in HR measurement is explored along with a readiness self-test.

Chapter 2, "The ROI Methodology," describes how the ROI process has evolved in recent years and how organizations are tackling this important issue. This chapter presents a brief summary of the model for those who are being introduced to the process for the first time.

Chapter 3, "Preparing for ROI," shows the initial analysis needed for an effective ROI evaluation process; it also explores when and where to use ROI.

Chapter 4, "Data Collection Issues," presents a variety of approaches to one of the most fundamental issues. Ranging from conducting surveys to monitoring performance data, the most common ways to collect data at all levels are described in this chapter. Useful tips and techniques to help select the appropriate method for a specific situation are presented.

Chapter 5, "Data Analysis," presents two of the most important aspects of the ROI methodology: isolating the effects of HR and converting the data to monetary values. Several strategies are presented to determine the amount of improvement directly linked to the HR program.

Also, several strategies to convert both hard and soft data to monetary values are presented along with many examples.

Chapter 6, "HR Costs and ROI," details specifically what types of costs should be included in the ROI formula. Different categories and classifications of costs are explored in this chapter, with the goal of developing a fully loaded cost profile for each ROI calculation. The actual ROI calculation is discussed with several issues surrounding its development and use.

Chapter 7, "Measuring Intangibles," is a brief chapter that focuses on nonmonetary benefits from the program. Recognizing that not all of the outcome measures from HR can or should be converted to monetary values, this chapter shows how intangible measures should be identified, monitored, and reported. Common intangible measures are examined.

Chapter 8, "Communicating and Using Evaluation Data," provides insight into the most appropriate and effective ways to communicate the results to a variety of target audiences. This chapter shows how to carefully select appropriate messages to meet the unique needs of important audiences. Next, strategies for using evaluation data are examined.

Chapter 9, "Taking a Sensible Approach to ROI," addresses a variety of issues needed to implement the ROI process effectively. By following logical steps and overcoming several hurdles, this chapter identifies the important issues that must be tackled for the ROI methodology to become a useful, long-lasting, and routine process.

What's on the CD-ROM?

Included with this book is a CD-ROM containing additional information about ROI, its application, and utilization. It is designed to complement the book and provide more detail for individuals interested in developing a deeper understanding of ROI. It also provides useful tools to streamline the implementation of the methodology. Specifically, the CD-ROM contains

■ a detailed case study that shows step by step how the ROI is developed and provides explanations along the way;

■ an extra chapter on ROI forecasting;

■ a self-assessment instrument to determine the status of HR measurement and accountability;

- various planning tools including a data collection plan, an ROI analysis plan, and a project plan with blank forms and completed examples;

- sample questionnaires for collecting data for ROI analysis;

- sample calculations for different part of the analysis;

- additional charts, tables, and figures;

- formulas formatted for spreadsheet use; and

- additional resources available on ROI from the authors.

Please enjoy!

—Jack J. Phillips
—Patricia Pulliam Phillips
info@roiinstitute.net

Acknowledgments

No book is a work of the authors alone. We have received much help along the way to make this book a reality. Many of the concepts, issues, and techniques have been developed from research and application. Our previous work on the ROI process provided the basic foundation for this book. In addition, many of our clients around the world have been valuable sources of helpful suggestions and allowed us to use their organizations to develop new tools and processes. Collectively, they have made this an important and rich new publication. To them we owe a debt of gratitude, particularly for their interest in exploring new frontiers of measurement and evaluation.

Two individuals who stand out as pioneers in the early development of HR measurement and evaluation have influenced us. First, in the training and development field, Donald Kirkpatrick has been a leader in the evaluation process. His ingenious framework for the levels of evaluation has provided the foundation for many evaluation processes and models. Second, Jac Fitz-enz blazed new trails in the development of HR measurement and HR benchmarking. Through his work at Saratoga Institute, Jac has made his mark on the HR field, clearly challenging us with the measurement imperative. We are fortunate to count Jac and Don among our colleagues and personal friends and are proud to continue their work through ours.

Special thanks go to Elsevier and the American Society for Training and Development for permission to use and adapt for the human-resources audience material from previously published books by the authors. Sources of materials are listed in the References and the Acknowledgments and Attributions at the end of the text.

We also owe thanks to the substantive and legal reviewers for the book, whose suggestions added depth and readability. The human-resources reviewers were Frances A Hume, SPHR, President Hume 'N Resources Consulting and Krist McFarland, SPHR, Vice President, Fugal Company. The legal reviewer was Brian E. Powers, Attorney, CEO, Caxton Growth Partners

Finally, we owe much appreciation to Joyce Alff, who has served us superbly in the managing and editing role for this publication and has kept us on schedule. Katherine Sanner and Jaime Beard provided excellent support in developing the manuscript. Jaime did a marvelous job of finalizing the manuscript. At SHRM, we are indebted to Laura Lawson, whose enthusiasm for this project made us work harder to produce a high-quality book.

CHAPTER 1

The Accountability Crisis

John Hamilton, senior vice president of the human resources (HR) department at Apex Business Products, was perplexed and a little confused after attending a meeting with the chief executive officer (CEO) Margarita Lopez. She had asked John to develop a plan to show the senior executive team the contributions of the HR function. Although the CEO fully supported the majority of HR programs and services, she questioned the value of a few of them and was concerned about comments from the senior team. As Lopez said, "Our senior execs wonder how much real value is contributed by the human resource function. Some of them think it could be outsourced or that parts of it could be eliminated altogether. What they want to see," she said, "is a more direct link between your programs and the bottom line."

As John reflected on the meeting, he was aware of the excellent HR programs at Apex. Some had even won awards from professional associations. He knew that the senior team placed value on the employees' annual feedback, which provided an assessment of job satisfaction, motivation, and commitment of the employees. This process had provided valuable information to help plan HR programs. John was also concerned that Lopez had mentioned making a link between HR program's and the company's bottom line. In other words, Lopez wanted to know about the return on investment (ROI) for HR programs. John was aware of the ROI concept but had not seen it applied to the HR function and wondered if it were even feasible.

John felt confused as he began to tackle the assignment. At the next senior staff meeting he would have to present his recommended plan for showing the value of the HR function to the senior management team. He knew he must have specific approaches to show the team to get buy-in. Otherwise he would have a tough challenge ahead as he entered the budgeting cycle.

John's story raises several questions:

■ What possibilities are available for John to show the HR contribution?

■ What specific types of measures are appropriate for an overall measurement process?

■ Is ROI feasible in this context?

■ How does ROI fit into the measurement mix?

■ Can ROI become a routine measure?

■ How can John win the support from the senior team?

■ How can a measurement system be implemented?

Most executives and HR professionals intuitively agree that investing in people and providing appropriate HR solutions and initiatives can pay off significantly for an organization. The problem is that this intuitive knowledge serves only as evidence, not proof, of payoff. Deciding which programs to invest in, how much to invest, and whether a particular HR program provides value is a haphazard process at many organizations.

This cloud of mystery around HR impact leaves some executives undecided about how much of a commitment to make in terms of time and resources to HR programs. Instead of making a continuous investment in the HR function, executives faced with a lack of tangible bottom-line results tend to resort to sporadic, inconsistent support of certain HR activities that seem to hold some promise in terms of helping the bottom line.

Defining ROI

The ROI methodology presented in this book can be used to show HR staff and other executives the monetary benefits directly connected to HR programs, particularly major programs that are highly visible, strategic, and expensive. This systematic, comprehensive measurement and evaluation process generates seven types of measures:

1. reaction and satisfaction with the HR program;

2. acquisition of knowledge and skills needed to implement the HR program;

3. application and implementation of the HR program;

4. business impact related to the HR program;

5. costs of the HR program;

6. return on investment in the HR program; and
7. intangible measures not converted to monetary values.

This balanced approach to measurement includes a technique to isolate the effect of the HR program. ROI is measured with the same formula that the finance and accounting staff would use to measure the return on investing in building equipment, for example.

About Terminology

Developing a book for the HR field always involves the difficult task of managing the vocabulary used in the field. Table 1 defines some key terms that are used throughout this book.

Major Influences on HR Accountability

Several developments—positive and negative—in recent years have influenced the need for additional HR accountability. All point toward a need to know more about the connection between investing in HR and the payoff of the investment.

The Triple Bottom Line

Much attention has focused recently on the concept of the triple bottom line. Not only must an organization be successful financially as demonstrated by traditional bottom-line measures, but it must also be successful with its employees and the external environment.

The employee "bottom line" is not readily defined, but it typically translates into the organization having favorable work conditions, treating employees fairly and equitably, and compensating them adequately, while fully recognizing the potential and capabilities of employees in a diverse environment. This measure has stimulated many organizations to search for ways in which to monitor, measure, and even value the employee contribution. Consequently, there is sometimes pressure to address this bottom line yet no clear direction of what it means. The "external environment" refers to the impact on and interaction with the community, the country, and the environment. Being a good corporate citizen and protecting the environment are two key issues.

Employer of Choice Phenomenon

Several publications and organizations recognize employers of choice every year or so. One of the most popular recognitions is *Fortune* magazine's annual list of the "100 Best Companies to Work For." In June 2004, the Great Place to Work Institute and the Society for Human Resource

Table 1. Some Key Terminology

Term	Definition
Program	A specific entity being evaluated. It may be a recruiting strategy, a new commission plan, a 6-month mentoring activity, a diversity initiative, a health-care cost containment measure, or a retention solution. "Program" is a more generic term than activity, solution, plan, initiative, intervention, or process.
Participant	Individuals directly involved in the program. The term "employee," "associate," or "stakeholder" could also be used. In many organizations, the term "participant" appropriately reflects those involved.
Stakeholder	All individuals or entities involved or interested in the program. The list of stakeholders may include the HR manager, participants, the organizer, and the key client, among others.
Client	The individual(s) or entity funding, initiating, requesting, or supporting a particular HR program. Sometimes referred to as the sponsor, it is the key group usually at the senior management level who cares about the program's success and is in a position to discontinue or expand the program.
Immediate Manager	Those in the organization who are one level above the participant(s) involved in the program. For some, the person in this position is the team leader; for others, it is the middle manager, but, most important, this person is the one with supervisory authority over the participant in the program.
Chief Executive Officer (CEO)	The top executive in an organization. The CEO could be a plant manager, division manager, regional executive, administrator, or agency head. The CEO is the top administrator or executive in the operating entity where the HR program is being implemented.

Management announced their own list of the "Best Small and Medium Companies to Work for in America." Many organizations strive to be included in the rankings. This status enables them to attract new applicants and retain valuable employees. Pursuing employer of choice status often drives HR programs to enhance the work environment and use this status to promote the organization to potential candidates. This phenomenon is driven by the employee retention issue that became such a critical topic during the 1990s.

This phenomenon has sometimes caused organizations to create too many programs that offer some fabulous new benefit, perk, or unparalleled opportunity. In some cases, the competition for the awards has placed strains on the HR function. Although there can be a significant value in improved retention and lower recruiting costs, the programs may not add enough value to overcome their costs. A measurement process is needed to show the payoff of these investments when they are significant.

HR Investment and Macro-Level Studies

Recent studies attempt to link the investment in HR to the ultimate payoff for the organization, which is often reflected in productivity or profitability. These macro-level studies, which cut across functions within organizations, attempt to correlate the organization's success with investments in HR.

Criticism of these studies suggests they do not show a significant relationship, or they fail to show a cause-and-effect relationship. For example, a profitable and productive firm may have ample funds to invest in a variety of programs to make the organization an attractive place to work. This finding does not, however, mean that the investment in the HR programs has led to the profitability.

Take, for example, QUALCOMM, an innovative, successful research and technology firm that holds the patents for much of the wireless communication technology. QUALCOMM has thousands of highly competent employees, and the company is consistently very profitable. The company invests heavily in building an employer of choice workplace. QUALCOMM is a regular on *Fortune's* "100 Best Companies to Work For." But which came first? Was it the employer of choice workplace that generated the profits, or was it the profits that enabled QUALCOMM to afford creating a workplace that merits distinction as an employer of choice? When reviewing macro-level data, such questions abound. Still, putting all criticism aside, these studies represent important insights into the power of investing in human capital.

Human Capital Management Focus

The concept of human capital is perhaps overused these days because so much has been written about how to monitor, measure, and value the human aspects of organizations. Nevertheless, much work still needs to be done with this important topic. In its early movement, much attention regarding human capital focused in the area of HR accounting—an attempt to account for the value of employees through traditional financial reporting methods. The difficulty lies in the methods for assigning a monetary value on the contribution or capability of human "assets." Although some progress was made, to date very few results and examples have been offered.

The human capital management trend also grew out of early benchmarking work of the 1980s as HR firms began to benchmark data and compare key indicators. A variety of measures on compliance, compensation, benefits, safety, retention, and absenteeism were developed. Today's human capital measurement mix contains those measures plus others, such as leadership, innovation, employee engagement, and learning. These new measures are critical to organizational growth and success. The challenge is to identify the appropriate blend of measures that reflects the status of human capital and enables decisions to be made about what to do with them.

Top Executive Demands

Senior executives are asking the HR function to show value. In some cases, HR is asked to show value or have its budget cut. Sometimes value must be shown before budgets are approved. In a few situations, this concern has led to outsourcing major parts or even all of the HR function. For years, HR escaped this level of scrutiny as employers invested in human capital on faith. They inherently believed that the more they invested in people, the more people would respond to the nature of their work. Today, executives are asking for data.

HR Disasters

Few organizations have the courage to admit to an HR disaster. The consequences of a flawed, ill-advised, or ineffective HR practice, program, or strategy can make excellent reading, particularly in the popular press. Unfortunately, a growing number of these stories are making their way into the HR professional press. An intriguing example is an exposé of the cost of an ill-advised HR strategy developed by Rent-A-Center. A decision to eliminate HR contributed to a $47 million payment required to settle litigation. The story is a classic one in which ill-advised practices and strategies went astray, not only costing a tremendous amount in direct payment but ultimately destroying the morale of the organization (Grossman, 2002). Although these types of disasters are reported more frequently in the press now, hundreds of others go unreported but probably represent tremendous mismanagement of human resources.

From an accountability perspective, HR staff has opportunities to add value. If, however, HR programs are mismanaged, the consequences can be negative. Appropriate data are needed to show how well programs are working and demonstrate their contribution to the organization. A comprehensive HR measurement system can help prevent some HR disasters, thus minimizing losses and changing the image of the HR function from one of a nice-to-have auxiliary department to one of a critical business function that contributes in a positive way to the organization's bottom line.

HR Technology

Perhaps no development has influenced the HR function as much as the advent of technology. Most HR transactions are now automated, including compensation administration, benefits administration, payroll, employee record keeping, recruiting, training, and orientation. Technology has eliminated the need for some HR staff. In certain cases, HR has been shifted to other areas (for example, finance or information technology), leaving some HR staff disconnected from where the work is often done.

On a positive note, technology has enabled collection of tremendous amounts of data that were previously unavailable. Employee and performance data can be organized, integrated, and reported in meaningful formats, thereby providing HR staff with the tools to measure the impact of the HR function and major HR initiatives.

HR Outsourcing

Outsourcing of HR services is an important trend among organizations during the last decade. Outsourcing means good *and* bad news. The good news is that many routine HR functions—not central to HR's primary mission or values—can be outsourced. This trend was initiated primarily in the payroll and employee-processing areas but has now expanded to include almost every part of the HR function. In some cases the entire HR staff and processes have been outsourced to external providers who offer the same services.

The bad news is that outsourcing is sometimes pursued for the wrong reasons. HR personnel fail to provide appropriate data and results to demonstrate the function's contribution to the organization. Sometimes outsourcing brings a short-term fix of immediate cost savings because fewer people earning lower salaries are doing the work. On a long-term basis, however, the result can be detrimental because satisfaction with the outsourced services can deteriorate.

The Accountability Trend of All Functions

It is somehow comforting to know that HR is not the only function being asked to show accountability. Many other functions are undergoing the same level of scrutiny, paradigm shifts, and changes. To be sure, they are all more accountable for expenditures.

Consider, for example, the information technology (IT) function. A few years ago, technology and IT groups had a blank check. They could implement almost any type of new technology, and it would be accepted because of the prevailing notion that technology was a competitive weapon that no firm could afford to be without. Unfortunately, many technology implementations were dismal failures that added tremendous costs but did not improve—or sometimes made worse—the very situations they were supposed to improve. In recent years, IT has been asked to show value even before investments are made and then carefully track the value to make sure that the projections are realized. This scrutiny has caused those responsible for implementing technology to measure not only the ROI but also a variety of other qualitative and quantitative measures thereby producing a balanced profile of success—the same process presented in this book.

A Paradigm Shift for HR Accountability

The factors described in the foregoing sections have had a tremendous effect on HR functions and their attempt to improve the effectiveness, impact, and the overall accountability of the HR function. Because of these influences, three important shifts have taken place in HR functions, as outlined in the sections that follow.

Measurement Trends

Table 2 shows some of the major measurement trends that are developing as a response to major influences on the HR function. These trends are shaping the way that HR functions react to major accountability issues. Not only are they prominent in the United States, but they are also reflective of the trends in major industrialized nations, as reported in surveys of HR practitioners and managers in more than 30 countries. These trends underscore the progress being made to bring accountability to HR.

Table 2. HR Measurement Trends

1. HR budgets are being justified based on HR measurement and evaluation data.

2. The strategic focus of many HR programs is requiring measurements before and after the program to predict and judge success.

3. More HR functions are being outsourced based on credible, balanced analysis of which functions would be best to be outsourced.

4. The interest in developing HR profit centers continues to progress.

5. There is increased success in measuring human capital in very difficult and soft areas such as leadership, innovation, and learning.

6. New HR executives have backgrounds or experience in business, finance, and operations.

7. Business-minded executives are transforming the way the HR function is being managed.

8. The HR staff is developing data to understand the relationship between HR measures and the outcomes of the organization.

9. The HR staff considers a balanced set of measures when evaluating a specific HR program, project, or solution.

10. Business evaluation is becoming more systematic, methodical, and proactive instead of sporadic and reactive.

11. Measuring ROI is growing in use as an HR evaluation tool.

Shift from Qualitative to Quantitative Measures

Figure 1 shows how measurement approaches have evolved in recent years. In the 1960s and '70s, most measurement was attitude and compliance oriented. This was the time when attitude surveys, case studies, and HR auditing measured the HR pulse. The concept of management by objectives was introduced. Next, during the 1970s and '80s, there was much focus on benchmarking and tracking key items and costs. Parallel with the advent of major benchmarking efforts, HR executives began to compare processes to others and monitor key indicators over which they had the most control.

During this time, there was also much focus on understanding the cost of HR and trying to control it in any way possible. Now, in the 1990s and continuing into the first decade of the 21st century, the focus is on value-add and impact. Measurement approaches attempt to show value and include financial measures. The concept of profit centers, scorecards, and ROI dominate the measurement landscape.

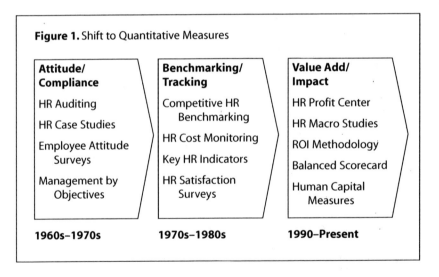

Figure 1. Shift to Quantitative Measures

Attitude/ Compliance	Benchmarking/ Tracking	Value Add/ Impact
HR Auditing	Competitive HR Benchmarking	HR Profit Center
HR Case Studies	HR Cost Monitoring	HR Macro Studies
Employee Attitude Surveys	Key HR Indicators	ROI Methodology
Management by Objectives	HR Satisfaction Surveys	Balanced Scorecard
		Human Capital Measures
1960s–1970s	**1970s–1980s**	**1990–Present**

This evolution of measurement reveals the current focus on showing the value of HR in ways that senior executives understand and accept. In some cases this means showing the actual measurement of ROI for specific programs or functions. The ROI relates to the other processes as well. For example, the ROI methodology is used to show the payoff of an HR program or solution designed to enhance or maintain the current level of a measure taken from the human capital measurement system or balanced scorecard system. The ROI methodology holds the most promise as a valuable and feasible measurement process that does not drain resources.

Shift to a Results-Based Approach

The approach to organizing, managing, and implementing the HR function has shifted from a traditional activity-based approach to a more results-based approach. Table 3 shows the major shifts that have occurred with HR programming. The trend has been away from a focus on generating programs and projects and inputs) to the current focus on results from the beginning of the process to the conclusion of the project.

Table 3. Paradigm Shift for a Results-Based Approach

Traditional Approach	Results-Based Approach
■ New programs are initiated by request or at the suggestion of any significant manager of a group.	■ New programs are initiated only after a legitimate need is established.
■ HR offers a multitude of programs in all areas.	■ The emphasis is on having fewer programs that offer great opportunity to make an impact.
■ Existing programs are rarely, if ever, eliminated or changed	■ Existing programs are regularly reviewed, revised, or eliminated when necessary
■ HR impact is measured by counting activities, hours of involvement, number of employees involved, and so forth.	■ HR impact is measured by determining the bottom-line impact of programs on the organization.
■ Management is involved only to a limited extent in the HR process	■ Management is extensively involved and collaborates in the HR process.
■ HR is viewed as a cost center.	■ HR is viewed as an investment in employees.
■ The HR staff is unfamiliar with operations issues.	■ The HR staff is very knowledgeable about operations.
■ The HR staff lacks knowledge of finance and business concepts.	■ The HR staff is versed in basic finance and business concepts.

Though the field of HR has been moving through this transition for many years, few organizations have shifted completely to a results-based approach for their HR functions. This results-based approach is the cornerstone of the methodology offered in this book.

Is HR Ready for Additional Measurement and Evaluation?

With all the influences, trends, and progress in measurement, one important question quickly comes to mind: Is HR ready for *more* measurement and evaluation? Are the influences in place in the organization to drive additional measurement? Figure 2 provides a checklist of issues that often are drivers for additional measurement. It may be helpful for you to answer the questions on the checklist now to gain an understanding of how these issues relate to your organization.

After you've responded to each item, add up your score using the scale at the top of the chart. The scale ranges from strongly disagree (1) to strongly agree (5).

Very high scores indicate tremendous pressures for increased accountability. For example, a total score in the 60–75 range indicates critical pressures for HR to measure results and show value; urgent action is needed. Scores in the 45–60 range indicate that there is a need for additional HR measurement although not to a point of crisis. Action will be needed in the near future to focus more resources and efforts on HR measurement.

In the 35–45 range, there is little pressure for additional measurement at the current time. Additional measurement may be useful to prevent some of the key issues and problems from surfacing in the future. A score below 30 indicates there is little concern about additional measurement and evaluation emphasis unless the HR staff wants to show value and express accountability on a proactive basis. This is the best time to get started. This brief assessment highlights some of the key issues about the need to invest in measurement and evaluation. The reality facing most HR executives is that additional investment—in terms of time and money—is needed to show the value of HR and increase accountability for HR programs and solutions.

Figure 2. Readiness for Additional HR Measurement and Evaluation[1]

Is Your Organization a Candidate for ROI Implementation?

Read each question and check of the most appropriate level of agreement
(1 = Disagree; 5 = Total Agreement)

	Disagree			Agree	
	1	2	3	4	5
My organization has a wide variety of HR programs and services.	❏	❏	❏	❏	❏
We have a large HR budget that reflects the interest of senior management.	❏	❏	❏	❏	❏
Our organization has a culture of measurement and is focused on establishing a variety of measures including HR.	❏	❏	❏	❏	❏
My organization is undergoing significant change.	❏	❏	❏	❏	❏
There is pressure from senior management to measure results of our HR initiatives.	❏	❏	❏	❏	❏
My HR function currently has a very low investment in measurement and evaluation.	❏	❏	❏	❏	❏
My organization has suffered more than one HR program disaster in the past.	❏	❏	❏	❏	❏
My organization has a new leader for HR.	❏	❏	❏	❏	❏
My management team would like to be the leader in HR processes.	❏	❏	❏	❏	❏
The image of our HR function is less than satisfactory.	❏	❏	❏	❏	❏
My clients are demanding that our HR processes show bottom-line results.	❏	❏	❏	❏	❏
My HR function competes with other functions within our organization for resources.	❏	❏	❏	❏	❏
My organization has increased its focus on aligning processes to the strategic direction of the company.	❏	❏	❏	❏	❏
My HR function is a key player in change initiatives currently taking place in my organization.	❏	❏	❏	❏	❏
We are required to prove the bottom-line value of our HR programs.	❏	❏	❏	❏	❏

The Payoff of ROI

The upside of investing in HR methodology can be great. Some of the payoffs, which are outlined in the following sections, can change the role, image, and success of the HR function.

Budgeting for HR

More HR executives have to justify their budgets in terms that managers understand. At times they must even project the value of specific programs or go back and determine the value of previous programs. Whether budgets are being approved or being considered for cuts, the pressure is there. Lack of data showing the connection between HR and its contribution will almost assuredly result in reduced funding. Conversely, showing value is one of the best business cases for justifying or enhancing an HR budget.

Preventing Disasters

A good measurement system can help prevent disasters because the system begins with a thorough analysis of the need for the HR program or initiative. It helps avoid unnecessarily initiating programs. Effective evaluation data provide constant feedback to show effective (or ineffective) a program is. In effect, evaluation keeps the program on track, allows for making adjustments, or eliminates the program quickly if it cannot add value. The important point is that appropriate evaluation data can prevent major disasters.

Eliminating Unnecessary or Ineffective Programs

The ROI methodology presented in this book is an excellent tool to determine if a program is adding appropriate value. If changes cannot be made, the course of action may be to eliminate or diminish the program. A sound, credible measurement process can provide data to determine necessary adjustments, even for politically sensitive, controversial programs. The important point is that without this type of measurement, unnecessary and ill-advised programs may continue to flourish, consuming resources and time, thereby, tarnishing the image of HR. Meanwhile, the problems that these programs are supposed to solve go unresolved.

Improving HR Processes

A comprehensive measurement process can improve implementation processes. As data are developed and used, ineffective parts of the program or solution are uncovered so that necessary changes can be made to improve the implementation processes. Barriers to success are always captured, revealing the processes that can be changed to ensure success. The enablers to success are also identified, revealing the factors that can be adjusted to drive more success.

Expanding or Implementing Successful Programs

Rigorous, bottom-line measures for HR can be used to justify expansion or application of HR programs. If a similar need exists for an HR program in another division, for example, an ROI evaluation can show that the program can be replicated in another area. Also, when a pilot program is undertaken, the measurement and evaluation process can determine if it should be implemented throughout the organization or in a particular division or area. Previously, HR pilot programs were evaluated based on subjective and reaction-level data. Now, these programs are being evaluated based on application, impact, and ROI data.

An important payoff for investing in measurement and evaluation is realized when a program identified as adding value is then implemented on a broader scale. The impact can be tremendous, adding value to the entire organization.

Strengthening Relationships with Key Executives and Administrators

No group is more important to the HR function than the senior executives. They allocate funds, commit resources, and show support for the HR function. They must understand the value and impact of the HR function. Executives need convincing data to accept HR as a business partner—one that they can invite to the table for important decisions and meetings. The ROI methodology can show the value of HR and strengthen this relationship with key executives. In addition, it can raise the respect and credibility of the HR staff, thereby shifting from the perception that HR is an expense to the perception that HR represents a solid investment.

Building Support from the Management Team

An important group that is often critical of HR's success is the management team, typically middle managers who often do not support HR to the extent that they should. This group has inherited some of the duties previously performed by the HR staff and need convincing evidence that HR programs are producing results. They need this evidence so that they will continue to commit time and resources to programs. Having an appropriate mix of data, including ROI, builds the level of commitment and support needed from this critical group. Without data to document the value added by HR programs, the management team tends to see HR as a necessary evil; with robust data, they can see HR as a catalyst to meeting their departments' goals.

Final Thoughts

This chapter highlighted many of the influences, trends, and issues that are driving the future direction of the HR function. Collectively, they build a compelling rationale for investing additional time and effort in measurement and evaluation. With the potential payoffs involved, it makes great business sense to invest more in HR measurement and evaluation.

Measurement and evaluation come in many varieties. ROI is the tool that satisfies most of the concerns outlined in this chapter. The challenge is to show the value in terms that executives and managers understand and appreciate. All HR stakeholders need to understand the value of this important function in the organization. Without measurement and evaluation, the consequences can be disastrous.

CHAPTER 2

The ROI Methodology

The previous chapter set the stage for increased investment in HR measurement and evaluation, and this chapter now makes the business case for using ROI as a part of the measurement process. You'll also have the opportunity to learn more about the rationale for the use of ROI methodology, its fundamental components, and ROI standards, which are essential for building the methodology's credibility and respect as a viable tool for the HR department.

The Essential Measurement Mix

The previous chapter described several approaches to HR measurement; pursuing all of them would be impossible and highly undesirable. The challenge is to select the appropriate mix for the organization given its needs, culture, resources, skills, and goals. The selection process usually involves a few measurement strategies that meet various needs of the stakeholders.

The measurement mix shown in Figure 3 is recommended as an appropriate mixture of measures that represent both qualitative and quantitative data taken from different sources at different times for different purposes. The first category is **attitudinal data**. In today's organizations, it is essential to have a finger on the pulse of employees to understand not only what satisfies them on the job, but also what motivates them and builds their commitment. Whether the issue is job satisfaction, organizational commitment, or employee engagement, employee feedback is routinely needed as a source of data.

The second category in the HR measurement mix is **comparative data**. Many organizations rely on benchmarking as a measurement tool, and it is important for the HR function also to be involved in major bench-

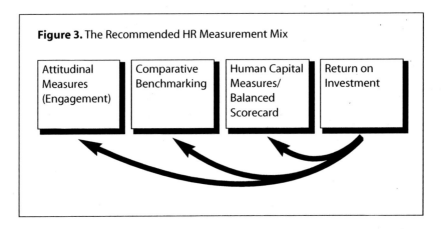

Figure 3. The Recommended HR Measurement Mix

| Attitudinal Measures (Engagement) | Comparative Benchmarking | Human Capital Measures/ Balanced Scorecard | Return on Investment |

marking efforts. These benchmarking studies may include comparing specific output measures (for example, turnover, absenteeism, or accidents) or process steps (for example, time to recruit a new employee), or particular cost items (such as cost per hire, training costs per employee). Although benchmarking shows executives the current level of commitment and progress when compared to other organizations, it does not provide insight into what is needed or the success of current HR strategies. Benchmarking merely compares the current organization with others that may represent best practices.

The third category is **human capital measures**. These are the important people-related indicators, initially tracked in the 1980s and enhanced considerably for the 21st century. Sometimes these measures are grouped into balanced scorecards that represent both qualitative and quantitative data. These measures are critical to the success of the organization and represent a variety of issues. For many high-growth and innovative organizations, human capital measures are critical indicators to monitor.

The fourth category is the **ROI methodology**, which compares the benefits of HR programs to the costs of those programs. Although other types of analyses show the general relationship between investing in HR and such outcomes as profits and productivity, most HR managers need a tool to show the impact of a particular program. The ROI methodology generates the data needed to convince a senior management team about HR's contribution. ROI is a new addition to the HR manager's measurement toolkit and is essential for showing managers the connection of HR to the bottom line and the impact of specific programs. As shown in Figure 3, this category links to the others. The ROI methodology is used to show the impact of a program or solution designed to enhance or maintain a specific human capital measure, a benchmarking statistic, or attitudinal data, such as organizational commitment.

Why ROI?

Several features of the ROI methodology make it an important measure for HR managers:

1. *ROI is the ultimate measure.* In the range of measurement possibilities, ROI represents the ultimate: a comparison of the actual cost of an HR program to its monetary benefits by using the same standard ratio accountants have used for years to show the ROI for equipment and buildings.

2. *ROI has been the elusive measure.* Many HR managers have long assumed that it was impossible to measure the return on investments in human resources. Recognizing that investment was essential and that human potential is an unlimited power, many HR leaders argued that ROI could and should not be applied to HR. The concept of ROI, therefore, has been surrounded by misconceptions, myths, and mysteries that have prevented many HR executives from pursuing it. Because of the increase in evidence showing otherwise, it is no longer an elusive measure.

3. *ROI has a rich history of application.* The ROI methodology is not a fad passing through the organization. It is a measure of accountability that has been in place for centuries. Wherever there is a significant expenditure, there is a need to know the financial impact of the expenditure. ROI will continue to be an economic measure in the future.

4. *Operating managers understand and relate to ROI.* Most managers in an organization have special training on how to manage the business. Some have business or management degrees or even master's degrees in business administration. These managers understand ROI and routinely use it to value other investments. They have a desire to have ROI data for major programs. They know how to use it, appreciate it, and support it.

5. *ROI builds excitement among stakeholders.* One of the most important sources of pride and satisfaction comes when the HR department

organizes, implements, or operates an HR program that results in a positive ROI calculation. No other measure can generate the amount of energy, excitement, and enthusiasm as ROI can, particularly when the ROI value exceeds expectations. Most stakeholders involved in HR programs intuitively believe that the programs add value, but ROI, as a measurement tool, confirms this intuition using a credible, validated process.

6. *ROI is a top executive requirement.* Thanks in part to the popular press and media attention to ROI as an evaluation tool, executives are suggesting, asking, requiring, and sometimes demanding that ROI be calculated for certain HR programs. Previously, executives assumed that ROI could not be developed based on logical and persuasive arguments from the HR staff. Now, these executives see many examples in which ROI is becoming an important part of the measurement mix. Consequently, in interviews, speeches, and articles, executives suggest that ROI should be required for HR expenditures. HR is treated the same as other business functions, and the HR department must produce value, as must the others. Gone are the days of blindly increasing HR investments with no clue as to their financial payoff.

These six factors sway many HR leaders to pursue ROI. It is the ultimate level of evaluation that is not only needed but is being required by some key stakeholders. More important, ROI provides different stakeholder groups important, balanced information about the success of an HR program.

Types of Data for ROI Methodology

At the heart of the ROI methodology are the varieties of data collected throughout the process and reported at different intervals. Some of the types of data are labeled levels because they reflect a successive effect in which one level affects the next.

Back in 1959, Donald Kirkpatrick (1998) described a four-level framework for evaluating training programs—a system that has become a standard among HR practitioners. His framework consists of the first four levels listed in table 4: reaction, learning, behavior (application/implementation), and results (business impact). The notion of evaluating HR contributions by calculating ROI—the fifth level of evaluation—was introduced subsequently (Phillips, 1997).

Table 4 lists and describes seven types of data that can be used to measure the overall success of HR programs. The first four levels roughly correspond to Kirkpatrick's four levels, and the last three relate to program cost data, ROI, and intangible data. As you move down the table to the higher levels of evaluation, the value ascribed to the data by the client increases. But, the degree of effort and cost of capturing the data for the higher levels of evaluation generally increases, too. Nevertheless, you can minimize these outlays with proper program planning and design.

Table 4. Types and Levels of Evaluation Data[2]

Level/Type	Measurement Focus
Reaction and Satisfaction	Measures participant satisfaction with the HR program and captures planned actions, if appropriate
Learning	Measures changes in knowledge, skills, and attitudes related to the HR program
Application/Implementation	Measures changes in on-the-job behavior or actions as the HR program is applied, implemented, or utilized
Business Impact	Measures changes in business impact variables
Costs	Measures the fully loaded costs of the HR program
Return on Investment (sometimes called Level 5 evaluation)	Compares monetary benefits to the costs of the HR program
Intangible Data	Measures that are not converted to monetary values

The following sections describe the various qualitative and quantitative measures that are listed in Table 4 and are basic to the ROI methodology described in this book.

Reaction and Satisfaction Data

The first category of data collected from an HR program is basic reaction data (level 1 evaluation). This is an immediate reaction to the program from a variety of key stakeholders, particularly those who are charged with the responsibility to make it work. At this level, a variety of basic satisfaction and reaction measures are taken, often representing 10 to 25 separate measures to gain insight into the reception and enthusiasm or disappointment with the HR initiative.

Learning Data

As employees become involved in an HR initiative, they must acquire information, absorb new knowledge, or learn new skills. In some cases as they attempt new skills, employees must feel confident in using those skills in the workplace setting. This level of measurement (level 2) focuses on the changes in knowledge and skill acquisition and details what employees have learned to make the HR program successful. Some HR solutions have a high learning component, such as those involved in training, development, education, and learning. Others may have a low learning component, such as policy changes, reward systems, and new benefits. In these situations, the learning involves understanding how processes work and what tasks or steps must be taken to make the program successful.

Application and Implementation Data

Application and implementation are key measures that show the extent to which employees have changed their behavior or implemented the HR program (level 3). These data reflect how employees take actions, make adjustments, apply new skills, change habits, implement specific steps, and initiate processes as a result of the HR program.

This is one of the most powerful categories of data because it uncovers not only the extent to which the HR program is implemented, but also details the reasons for lack of implementation in some cases. At this level, barriers and enablers to application and implementation are detailed and provide a complete profile of success at the various steps of implementation.

Business Impact Data

For every behavior change achieved or action taken in application and implementation, there is a consequence. This consequence can be described in one or more measures representing an impact on the employee's own work environment, as an impact directly on his or her team, or as an impact in other parts of the organization.

This level of data (level 4) reflects the specific business impact and may include measures such as output, quality, costs, time, job satisfaction, and customer satisfaction that have been influenced by the application and implementation of the program. A direct link between business impact and the program must be established for the HR program to drive business value. At this level of analysis, a technique must be used to isolate the effects of the HR program from other influences that may be driving the same measure. It is imperative that the HR department be able to answer the question: "How do you know it was your HR program that caused the improvement and not something else?"

HR Program Cost Data

This level of data reveals the actual cost of the HR solution or program. A fully loaded cost profile reflects all of the direct costs (for example, the cost of photocopying materials just for that program) and indirect costs (for example, the support needed from the Accounting Department to support the program) of the specific HR function, project, solution, or program.

Return-on-Investment Data

This level of measure compares the monetary value of the business impact measures to the actual cost of the HR program. This is the ultimate level of accountability and represents the financial impact directly linked with the program expressed as a benefit-cost ratio or return-on-investment percentage. HR practitioners often refer to this measure as the "fifth level of evaluation" as a way of building upon Kirkpatrick's four levels of evaluation.

Intangible Data

The seventh type of data—intangible benefits—consists of measures that intentionally are not converted to monetary value. To develop the ROI, you must convert business impact measures to monetary value. In some cases, however, converting certain measures to monetary values simply is not credible. When such is the case, the data are listed as an intangible but only if linked to the HR program.

Figure 4 shows five of the seven types of data arranged as levels in a chain of impact that is necessary if the HR program is to drive business value. Reaction leads to learning, which leads to application, which leads to business impact, and ultimately to ROI. At the business impact level, the effects of the HR program must be isolated from other influences. Also, business impact data must be converted to monetary value and compared to the cost of the HR program to develop the ROI. Intangible benefits are often the business impact data that cannot be credibly converted to monetary value. It is important for all stakeholders to understand this chain of impact. It is a novel, yet pragmatic, way to show the consequences of HR programs.

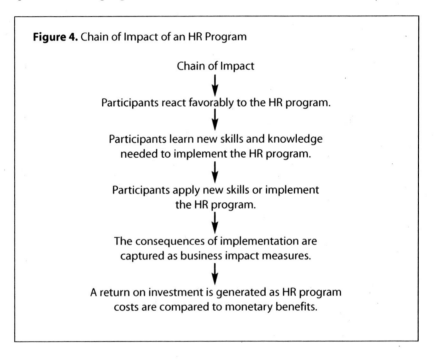

Figure 4. Chain of Impact of an HR Program

Chain of Impact

Participants react favorably to the HR program.

Participants learn new skills and knowledge needed to implement the HR program.

Participants apply new skills or implement the HR program.

The consequences of implementation are captured as business impact measures.

A return on investment is generated as HR program costs are compared to monetary benefits.

An Example

An example is helpful to understand how the chain of impact works. It explains the different type of data and their importance. Table 5 shows data collected from an evaluation of an employee suggestion system in a large electric utility. This new HR program represents a typical employee suggestion system design in which employees are rewarded with cash payments if a suggestion is accepted, implemented, and cost savings are realized. The table reflects how the data are developed through the chain of

Table 5. Example of Types and Levels of Data

Employee Suggestion System

Type of Data	Data Collection Method	Data Source	Timing	Results
Reaction and Satisfaction (Level 1)	Questionnaire	Employees	At the end of the announcement meeting	4.3 out of 5 rating on usefulness, fairness, and appropriateness
Learning (Level 2)	Questionnaire	Employees	At the end of the announcement meeting	4.1 out of 5 rating on under-standing the procedures, case documentation, award determi-nation, and notification
Application and Implementation (Level 3)	Monitor Records	Employee Suggestion System	Annually	10.4% participa-tion rate
Business Impact (Level 4)	Monitor Business Performance	Employee Suggestion System	Annually	$1.52 million in 2 years
Cost	Monitor Records	Cost Statements	Annually	$2.1 million cost in 2 years
ROI (Level 5)	—	—	—	-28%
Intangibles	Questionnaire	Sample of Employees	Annually	Increased cooperation, commitment to the organiza-tion, pride of ownership, and employee satisfaction

impact. At level 4 (business impact), the results look very promising as $1.52 million in benefits has been achieved in a two-year timeframe.

However, the ROI reveals a negative value because the operational costs ($2.1 million) exceed the monetary benefits during the same two-year period. ROI presents the ultimate accountability as the monetary benefits ($1.52 million) are compared to the cost ($2.1 million):

$$\frac{\$1.52 \text{ million} - \$2.1 \text{ million}}{\$2.1 \text{ million}} \times 100\% = -28\% \text{ ROI}$$

This evaluation underscores the importance of taking the analysis all the way to ROI for certain programs. If the evaluation had stopped at business impact, level 4, the financial value of the suggestion system would not be developed, only the business impact.

As shown in Table 5, the employee suggestion system results in a negative ROI (-28%). Nevertheless, a negative ROI does not always result in an adverse consequence. Some benefit is derived from this program as behavior is changed and the intangibles are linked with the program. As shown, the intangible benefits include important measures such as increased cooperation, organizational commitment, pride of ownership, and employee satisfaction. In such cases, a negative ROI may be accept-

Figure 5. The ROI Methodology[3]

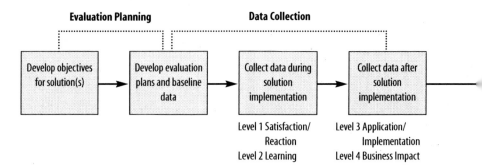

Source: Phillips, J., Stone, R., and Phillips, P. 2001. The Human Resources Scorecard: Measuring Return on Investment. Boston: Butterworth-Heinemann.

able. However, if a positive ROI was expected, then a negative ROI is unacceptable.

The ROI Methodology

The ROI model encompasses the seven types of data in a consistent and systematic way. Figure 5 shows the systematic approach for capturing data, processing and analyzing data, and reporting results.

As can be seen in the figure, the activities comprising the ROI methodology fall into four basic categories:

- evaluation planning;
- data collection;
- data analysis; and
- reporting.

Planning for Evaluation

The first step in planning is to develop objectives that reflect all the various types of data. Ideally, for major programs, objectives should be set at

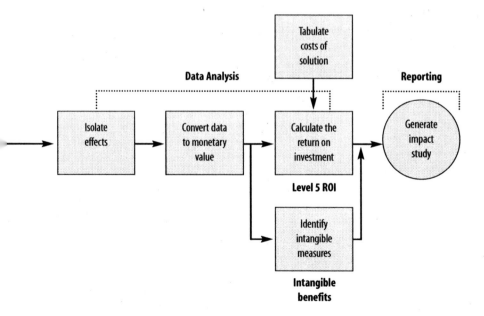

each level and linked to baseline data, if available. The challenge is to push the objectives to higher levels beyond reaction and learning objectives to include application, impact, cost, and even ROI. Objectives provide the necessary focus for program designers and the direction needed for program organizers. In addition, objectives show the participants, usually employees, what specifically should be accomplished with the HR program. Higher levels of objectives also provide program sponsors with meaningful data by which to judge the feasibility and initial effectiveness of the HR program.

The second part of the planning process involves developing the planning documents. Three documents are recommended although they can be combined into a single plan. The three documents include a data collection plan, ROI analysis plan, and a communication and implementation plan. Additional detail on evaluation planning is presented in Chapter 3.

Data Collection

As Figure 5 showed, data collection involves four different types of data that reflect the first four levels of evaluation (see Table 4). During the implementation of the program, reaction, satisfaction, and learning data are collected. After the program is implemented, application, implementation, and business impact data are captured on a follow-up basis. Data collection methods used to capture the first four levels of data include questionnaires, observations, interviews, focus groups, and business performance monitoring. These common data collection methods capture a variety of qualitative and quantitative data. Additional information on data collection is presented in Chapter 4.

Data Analysis

To analyze the collected data, it is necessary to isolate the effects of the HR program, convert the data to monetary values, capture HR costs, calculate ROI, and identify intangible measures. Each step is described briefly here.

Isolating the Effects of the HR Program. Although difficult and challenging, it is necessary to determine the business contribution of the HR program. Fortunately, there are many ways by which this can be accomplished. The typical methods used to isolate the effects of the HR program from other factors include the use of control groups, time series analysis, and expert estimation. Some of these techniques are research focused, whereas others are more subjective but are still valuable. These techniques are described in more detail in Chapter 5.

Converting Data to Monetary Values. Another important challenge is converting business data to monetary value. Whether hard or soft data, there is pressure to show the actual monetary value of data. If the actual ROI is needed, data must be converted to monetary value. A variety of techniques are available to make this conversion including the use of standard values, which are almost always available, as well as the use of records, expert input, external databases, and estimations.

For short-term programs, only the first year's benefits are used to represent one year of improvement. For long-term programs, longer time periods are used. The important challenge is to use the most conservative approach, even one that is more conservative than that used by the chief financial officer. Chapter 5 offers more details.

Representing HR Costs. Monitoring the cost of the HR program is essential and must be represented by a fully loaded cost profile. Fully loaded costs should represent both direct and indirect categories including analysis and development costs, implementation costs, the costs of time for those involved in the program, and overhead costs. You can access cost data using cost statements, cost guidelines, benchmark data, and estimations. More details on costs are included in Chapter 6.

Calculating ROI. The ROI may be calculated using either the benefit-cost ratio or the ROI formula. The benefit-cost ratio (BCR) is defined as the total monetary benefits for the period of time selected divided by the fully loaded costs of the HR program:

$$\text{Benefit-Cost Ratio (BCR)} = \frac{\text{HR Program Benefits}}{\text{HR Program Costs}}$$

The ROI, although similar to the BCR, uses net benefits divided by costs. (The net benefits are the program benefits minus program costs.) In the formula form, the ROI is:

$$\text{ROI (\%)} = \frac{\text{HR Program Benefits - HR Program Costs}}{\text{HR Program Costs}} \times 100$$

or

$$\text{ROI (\%)} = \frac{\text{HR Program Net Benefits}}{\text{HR Program Costs}} \times 100$$

This is the same basic formula used for evaluating capital investments where the ROI is traditionally reported as earnings divided by investment. In the context of HR, earnings equate to net HR program benefits (in monetary benefits), and investment equates to the fully loaded HR program costs.

The BCR and the ROI present the same general information but with slightly different perspectives. An example illustrates the use of these formulas. An HR program designed to reduce absenteeism produced benefits of $581,000 at a cost of $229,000. Therefore, the benefit/cost ratio is:

$$BCR = \frac{\$581,000}{\$229,000} = 2.54 \text{ (or 2.5:1)}$$

As this calculation shows, for every $1 invested, $2.54 in benefits is returned. In this example, net benefits are $581,000 - $229,000 = $352,000. Thus, the ROI is:

$$ROI\% = \frac{\$352,000}{\$229,000} \times 100 = 154\%$$

This means each $1 invested in the HR program returns $1.50 in net benefits after accounting for costs. The benefits are usually expressed as annual benefits for short-term programs, representing the amount saved or gained for a complete year after the HR program has been implemented. Although the benefits may continue after the first year, the impact usually diminishes and is omitted from calculations in short-term situations. For long-term projects, the benefits are spread over several years. This conservative approach is used throughout the application of the ROI methodology described in this book. Additional information on the ROI calculations is presented in Chapter 6.

Identifying Intangible Measures. Intangibles are measures directly linked to the program and developed at different timeframes. Although intangible benefits are not converted to monetary value, they represent important data, often having as much perceived value as the tangible ROI calculation. Typical intangible data include job satisfaction, organizational commitment, teamwork, customer service, conflicts, and stress. This list is not meant to imply that these measures cannot be converted to monetary value. In most organizations, these items are not converted because the conversion cannot be accomplished credibly. Additional details on intangibles are presented in Chapter 7.

Reporting

The final step in the ROI methodology entails reporting the data to the many stakeholders who need HR success data. The challenge at this step is to determine the appropriate target audience, the information that is needed, the communication media that fit the situation, and the timing of presentation. Collectively, you must address these issues to have a systematic process for reporting data. Chapter 8 presents additional detail on reporting.

ROI Standards

Every process or model must have operating standards to be reproducible, accurate, and sustainable. The operating standards for this process show how data are developed, processed, utilized, and reported using very conservative principles. The conservative approach builds respect, credibility, and buy-in from the management group. The operating standards for the ROI methodology are labeled guiding principles, which support decision making and replication of the ROI methodology. The 12 ROI guiding principles are:

1. *When a higher-level evaluation is conducted, data must be collected at lower levels.* A balanced data set is needed that represents all seven types of data and provides a complete profile of success using both qualitative and quantitative data. Some data represent lower levels of evaluation, and others represent higher levels. Lower-level data are needed to understand the dynamics of the process and provide insight into problem areas and opportunities. For example, an adverse reaction at the first level can cause the program to fail from the beginning, but this will not be known unless an adequate amount of reaction data is collected. Also, many HR projects have a tendency to deteriorate during application and implementation. Collecting data at this level provides insight into the barriers and enablers so adjustments can be made.

2. *When an evaluation is planned for a higher level, the previous level of evaluation does not have to be comprehensive.* This is a resource-saving principle designed to keep costs at a minimum. No organization has unlimited resources for funding measurement and evaluation projects. Shortcuts must be used, costs must be controlled, and steps

must be taken to keep time commitments to a minimum. When short-cuts are taken, as a general rule, it is best to take them at the lower levels. The corollary to this principle is to use the most comprehensive analysis at the highest level of evaluation pursued.

3. *When collecting and analyzing data, use only the most credible sources.* Credibility is an important concern in HR measurement and evaluation data. When data are presented, credibility will be a primary issue that must be addressed to build respect and support for an impact study. One critical determinant of credibility is the source of the data. Sources must be identified that are most credible for the particular issue, and this can vary with studies and with groups. In some studies the management team is very credible; in others, they are not as credible for a particular item. The important point is to evaluate each data item and determine the most credible source for that particular item.

4. *When analyzing data, choose the most conservative method among alternatives.* In some cases there is more than one way to conduct a specific analysis. For example, when isolating the effects of an HR program, more than one method may be used. When this is the case, it is recommended that the most conservative one be used (the one that generates the lowest ROI). This principle assumes that both processes are equally credible. The net effect of this principle is to eliminate doubt and error by understating rather than overstating results.

5. *At least one method must be used to isolate the effects of the HR program.* This principle represents a critical challenge with HR projects. The amount of the improvement in a specific data item that is related to the project must be isolated from other influences. Although there are a variety of techniques, one technique must always be used. Otherwise, the impact study is not credible because there is no direct linkage between the program and impact. The default method for isolation is the use of estimates from individuals who know the process best. When all else fails, estimation is used. Because of this situation, estimation may be the method used in the majority of settings.

6. *If no improvement data are available for a particular population or from a specific source, it must be assumed that little or no improvement has occurred.* No data equals no improvement. This is perhaps

the most conservative of the guiding principles. If participants do not respond to questionnaires, surveys, action plans, or other data collection methods, it is assumed that they have achieved no value with the HR program. Also, if the participants are no longer in their job assignments or in the organization, it is assumed that they did not achieve success with the HR program. Realistically, some value may have been developed by the non-respondents, particularly if they are still on the job, or when there is a departure, the employee may have been successful before he or she left the organization. This guiding principle exerts much pressure to obtain as much data as possible from credible sources, a factor that is at the heart of the implementation of the ROI methodology.

7. *Estimates of improvement should be adjusted (discounted) for the potential error of the estimate.* Sometimes estimates will have some error. The amount of error is eliminated in the analysis. By using the concept of confidence estimates, an error range is created and the low side of the error range is used, thus compensating for any doubt or error associated with the estimate. This guiding principle builds credibility because the results are understated instead of overstated.

8. *Extreme data items and unsupported claims should not be used in ROI calculations.* Occasionally, extreme data items (sometimes called outliers) appear to be connected to the program or, in some cases, may be directly connected. Because they are extreme, they are omitted from the ROI analysis. It is important to protect the integrity of the ROI calculation, and it is important for key stakeholders to understand that the payoff is not generated on extreme values. Extreme data items are reported in other parts of an impact study but not in the ROI calculation. Also, unsupported claims are not used in the ROI analysis. For example, if participants do not show the source of data or how they developed monetary value, the claim is omitted from the ROI calculation although it may be included in the impact study in another section. These two issues in this guiding principle add credibility to the analysis.

9. *Only the first year of benefits (annual) should be used in the analysis of short-term HR programs and solutions.* The concept of ROI is an annual concept, so one year's worth of data is always needed. To be conservative, only the first year is used for HR programs that are

short-term in their implementation. "Short-term" is defined as the length of time it takes to implement the program with a particular individual or group. If it takes 10 days to implement a new reward system, then it is a short-term program, and the ROI should be developed based on one-year benefits. However, a two-year continuous mentoring and coaching process is a long-term solution, and a longer period is needed. The important point is to be conservative by using a number of years that is fair and at the same time as short as possible. This number should be established before the study is initiated and with input from the finance and accounting staff, if possible.

10. *Use fully loaded HR program costs for the ROI analysis.* Costs represent the denominator of the ROI calculation. Both direct and indirect costs should be included. Indirect costs are not normally included by some stakeholders. For example, the chief financial officer may argue that the use of meeting room space for meetings connected with an HR program implementation should not be charged because the meeting room is a fixed cost. However, a conservative approach is to account for all expenditures even on an allocated or prorated basis. Including this cost in the analysis may not materially affect the ROI calculation, but it is an important gesture that may be necessary to gain additional respect for the methodology.

11. *Intangible benefits are measures that are purposely not converted to monetary values.* An important issue that can affect the ROI calculation and the credibility of an ROI study is the issue of converting data to monetary values. Some data are considered to be soft (or intangible) and cannot (or should not) be converted to monetary value. If the conversion cannot be made on a credible basis in the specific setting, the data item is left as an intangible benefit. The key issue surrounds the method used to make the conversion. Specific rules are developed to decide when a measure should be converted to monetary value or when it should be left as an intangible. Rules are developed so that two different researchers or evaluators can arrive at the same decision regarding the conversion of intangible data.

12. *Communicate the results of the ROI analysis to all key stakeholders.* Communicating data to the appropriate audience groups is critical. The first step in this process is to identify the stakeholders who need the information and then ensure that these and other groups receive

the desired information using the most effective medium at the right time with the appropriate content. You should include four key stakeholders in your communications: (1) the individual participants who are charged with implementing the HR program; (2) the immediate managers of the participants; (3) the key client or sponsor of the HR program; and (4) other HR team members.

These macro-level guiding principles ensure that the ROI methodology is consistent, routine, and standardized. At the same time, they keep costs low and credibility high. They are essential to obtain the appropriate buy-in and support needed for the ROI methodology. The guiding principles are explained in more detail throughout the book.

Final Thoughts

This chapter began with the reasons for implementing ROI methodology. Next, the different types and levels of data were explained, which provide the framework for the ROI analysis. Step by step, the ROI methodology was explored, showing how the seven types of data are generated, analyzed, and communicated. Finally, the guiding principles of ROI were described, showing how consistency and standardization are used to make the process realistic, replicable, and credible.

CHAPTER 3

Preparing for ROI

Preparing the organization and the HR department for ROI measurement invites a few challenges. Therefore, reserve ROI analysis for certain HR programs in the organization. This chapter explores how to select programs for ROI analysis and describes the preparations necessary to begin each ROI study.

When to Use ROI

Every HR program should be evaluated in some way even if the evaluation involves only reaction/satisfaction data collected from a select group of stakeholders. Including evaluation as a part of every HR program is a fundamental requirement. Reaction/satisfaction data alone are sufficient for evaluating many HR programs. Nevertheless, when appropriate and feasible, you should collect additional data to conduct higher-level evaluations.

Decide upon the appropriate level of evaluation for each HR program when the program is initiated, realizing that the evaluation level may change throughout the life of the program. For example, you can evaluate a new-employee orientation program with reaction/satisfaction (level 1) and learning (level 2) data. The objective at this point is to ensure that employees learn what they need to know to be successful and have the appropriate impressions about the organization. Later, a follow-up evaluation may be implemented to determine if the new employees are using the information provided in the orientation and if they are progressing appropriately based on what they have learned during orientation. Such a follow-up evaluation is an application/implementation evaluation (level 3).

If the cost of the new employee orientation rises, some managers may question the value of the process and push the evaluation to higher levels.

To carry out level 4 or 5 evaluations, it may be necessary to redesign the new-employee orientation program. You can then compare the redesigned version to the previous version to see if there is a difference. The difference may be evaluated with business impact data (level 4) or ROI (level 5) or both. During the life of a particular program or function, the desired level of evaluation may change.

Because of the resources required and the realistic barriers for implementing ROI, use the methodology only for certain programs. You should consider several criteria, outlined in the following sections, when selecting an evaluation level for HR programs.

Recommended Programs for Evaluation at Lower Levels

Reaction and satisfaction evaluation (level 1) can suffice as the only level of evaluation for short programs, such as briefings, policy introductions, or general information distributed to employees. If satisfaction with the program is critical, ongoing assessment of reaction may be appropriate. For example, a routine assessment of reaction to a telecommuting program is appropriate to determine the extent to which employees continue to perceive the program as fair, responsive, appropriate, and helpful.

Learning evaluation (level 2) is appropriate when it is essential for employees to acquire specific knowledge or skills presented in an HR program. Learning evaluations may be helpful for certain compliance initiatives in which employees must learn how and why the organization complies with a variety of regulations. These data are also critical for safety and health programs that safeguard employees' welfare. Participants in safety programs must know correct procedures and practices. Learning evaluation is also helpful for certain policies that employees must know, such as diversity, value systems, and routine policies and procedures that are critical to the job and the organization.

Application and implementation evaluation (level 3) is necessary when it is important for employees to perform in a particular way on the job as a result of an HR program. For example, if employees are required to deliver a certain level of customer service based on job design, reward systems, or training and development, it may be helpful to monitor employees to be sure that they are delivering the proper service. Spot audits or observations of employees interacting with customers can often ensure they are applying appropriate behavior on the job. If safety and security are issues, it is absolutely essential that key programs be evaluated at level 3 to make certain that employees are doing what they are supposed to do or reacting properly under particular circumstances.

The tradeoff in deciding which level of evaluation is appropriate is not only a test of the ideal, but also a tradeoff with resources available and the amount of disruption allowed in the organization. Because most data collection at this level disrupts the organization in some way, the evaluation must be balanced with the time, effort, and resources that can be committed to the process. Most organizations fall short of the ideal evaluation and settle for a feasible approach within the existing constraints.

Recommended Programs for Impact and ROI Analysis

Programs taken to the levels of business impact and ROI analysis are special ones for which it is important to understand the contributions they make to the organization. Among the criteria you should consider when selecting programs to evaluate with business impact and ROI data are the following:

- expected lifecycle of the HR program;
- importance of the program to strategic objectives;
- cost of the program;
- time commitment of participants;
- visibility of the program;
- extent of management interest.

Table 6 lists some programs often taken to these levels of analysis. The table represents both impact and ROI analysis, but it is helpful to review the distinction between the two levels. Sometimes the business impact of the program is desired without the subsequent ROI analysis. For example, a program designed to improve job satisfaction may be evaluated only at the business impact level. In that case, you'll want to develop the direct link between the HR program and job satisfaction. The ROI methodology requires that you develop the monetary benefits of the program and compare them to the costs of the program. Because of the difficulty in converting job satisfaction data to monetary value, you may not wish to pursue ROI analysis in this example.

Expected Lifecycle of the Program. The first criterion in selecting programs for business impact and ROI analysis is the length of time the program is in existence (lifecycle). Some HR programs are one-time opportunities designed to react to a particular issue or tackle a particular

---

Table 6. Programs Suitable for ROI or Business-Level Analysis

- Employee Relations Program
- Career Development Programs
- Competency Systems
- Diversity Programs
- E-Learning Programs
- Executive Coaching
- Management Development
- Gain Sharing Programs
- Leadership Development
- Organization Development

- Orientation Systems
- Recruiting Strategies
- Retention Improvement
- Safety and Health Programs
- Self-Directed Teams
- Skill-Based/Knowledge-Based Compensation
- Technology Implementation
- Total Quality Management
- Wellness/Fitness Initiatives

---

problem in the organization. These programs are intended to be brief, and ROI analysis may not be necessary. For example, an early retirement offer with a short deadline or mandatory ethics training for all employees may be one-shot programs. Conversely, some programs seem to exist forever. For example, a new-employee orientation program will always be needed as long as there are new employees. Consequently, at some point in its lifecycle, it may be helpful to conduct a comprehensive analysis. Nortel Networks pursued an ROI evaluation of its orientation program because it was considered a permanent fixture.

Linkage to Strategic Initiatives Objectives. Another important issue is the linkage of the program to strategic initiatives or operational goals. A strategic program is one designed to address specific strategic objectives. These programs are so important that they should be subject to a high level of scrutiny.

For example, a major customer service initiative designed to support a strategic goal of improving customer satisfaction may be a candidate for ROI. BellSouth Corporation evaluated one of its major customer service HR programs because it was linked to several strategic initiatives. Other programs may be operationally focused, adding significant impact to the organization's bottom line. For example, workout programs, similar to those instituted at General Electric where managers tackled particular issues and problems in a formal development effort may be suitable candidates for ROI. These programs are designed to add value and, consequently, should be subjected to ROI analysis to see if they are adding appropriate value as intended. A large metropolitan transit system pursued an ROI study on an absenteeism reduction program for bus drivers because of the operational problems related to excessive absenteeism.

Cost of the Program. Expensive programs need a comprehensive level of analysis to ensure that they are adding appropriate value. For example, in a large commercial bank, an expensive leadership development program costing $100,000 per candidate was subjected to ROI analysis to show the actual value, using a sample of participants. The board of directors wanted this evaluation because of perceived excessive costs. Another example: The Royal New Zealand Navy pursued an ROI study on a retention bonus plan for marine engineers because the plan cost the Navy $4 million. In contrast, however, a tuition reimbursement program for off-the-job education programs directly related to the job utilized by only 3% of the employees may not be a candidate for ROI analysis.

Time Commitment. Programs that involve much time are also candidates for business impact and ROI analysis. If employees must take a great deal of time away from their jobs to attend meetings and learning sessions, it can be helpful to determine if the process is adding value.

For example, at Allied Irish Bank, senior executives questioned the value of a 360-degree feedback process because it required so much of the managers' time. The managers complained about filling out the many forms, receiving feedback data, and attending training sessions and meetings to analyze and understand the process. This excessive time caused executives to question the value of the program.

Visibility of the Program. Highly visible or controversial programs often generate a need for accountability at higher levels. Because such programs can stimulate concern among their critics, they require a higher level of accountability. For example, a wellness and fitness center built for employees at a major automotive manufacturing complex was selected for ROI analysis based on its visibility. Sometimes managers and shareholders question the value of a high-profile project or program, thus elevating the evaluation to the business impact or ROI level.

Management Interest. The extent of management interest is often the most critical issue in driving programs for impact and ROI analysis. Senior executives have concerns about some programs but not all of them. Based on feedback they receive or their own perceptions of the program, they want this level of accountability applied.

For example, a National Aeronautics and Space Administration (NASA) executive recently required an impact analysis for one of its education programs, the NASA Faculty Fellowship Program. Senior administrators wanted to know if the program was adding value to NASA and to the universities. The good news is that there are only a few programs where these concerns exist. Even if the other criteria do not apply, it may be helpful or even necessary to elevate the evaluation to these levels to satisfy executive concerns. So-called "soft" programs that deal with diversity, motivation, empowerment, and communication are often scrutinized closely by executives who are not clear about the programs' value to the organization.

Programs Unsuitable for ROI

To determine which programs are not suitable candidates for impact and ROI analysis, one could apply criteria that are essentially the opposites of those used to select programs for higher levels of analysis. However, other factors are often helpful in sorting out those that should not be considered for business impact and ROI evaluation.

In some cases, developing an ROI value could send an unintended negative signal. For example, if an ROI evaluation were conducted on a sexual harassment prevention program, a non-supervisory female employee, who may be a potential victim of sexual harassment herself, would probably not appreciate ROI data. Reporting an ROI in dollars and cents may give the impression that the organization is only pursuing this program because there is a monetary payoff, ignoring the fact that the activity is illegal and unethical. Therefore, the decision of whether to conduct a business impact evaluation or an ROI analysis for an HR program is important. Nevertheless, the general criteria that lead to these levels of analysis are often very similar.

Programs required by external regulation or by executive mandate are often not good candidates for ROI analysis. Compliance programs exist for a variety of non-economic reasons, and the range of options to correct problems or improve programs may be limited. It is unlikely that such programs could be modified significantly, making evaluation at this level frustrating or pointless. If change is not an option, evaluation is probably useless. With limited resources available for this level of analysis, these programs do not typically make the grade, unless senior executives want to pursue it for some reason.

Programs of short duration are not appropriate for impact and ROI analysis, either. For a program to add value, there often has to be a change in behavior or a significant change in actions. Short-duration programs do not typically drive this type of change.

HR programs that involve only a small group of people are not necessarily good candidates for this analysis. The time and costs for the program may be insignificant.

Job-related programs may not be good candidates for ROI analysis. These include entry-level training, such as technical skills necessary for job or programs designed to cover basic policies, practices, and procedures. These are necessary for on-the-job success, and their value rarely comes into question.

Finally, programs that are important to the value systems of the organization or those designed to make social and political statements are usually not good candidates for ROI analysis. These programs are in place for a variety of non-economic reasons, and the actual payoff to the organization in the short term is often not an issue.

Selecting the First Project for ROI Analysis

ROI analysis is new to many organizations, and the use of this tool can be extremely powerful. ROI analysis, however, can also reveal ineffective programs and identify the reasons for failures. Also, ROI analysis requires skills that must be developed through trial and practice.

With these factors in mind, a few requirements for first-time projects are often helpful. The first requirement is simplicity; it is helpful to tackle a very simple project for which the issues are few and the scope is narrow. This focus helps the HR staff achieve early success and undertake ROI analysis for more complicated and sensitive issues later.

Another issue is perception of the project in terms of current success. It is helpful to tackle projects that appear to be successful based on current feedback. Training programs that are already considered to be successful help ensure that the first ROI study has a positive ROI. Nothing is more discouraging than having the first study generate a negative ROI, possibly deflating the enthusiasm of the entire group.

Another issue is to avoid programs that are controversial, political, or sensitive in nature. These programs often have hidden agendas and political issues that make it difficult to tackle as a first project. A study organizer might get caught in the crossfire between feuding executives. Although these programs can be addressed later with the process, it is best to avoid them in the early stages.

Finally, it is helpful to avoid a program that is a pet project of a senior executive. The program may have critics or supporters that can influence the data, conclusions, and recommendations. Considering these additional criteria can help avoid frustration that comes from the early use of the ROI methodology. It can also help build confidence in a methodology that can eventually be used to tackle any type of program, in any setting, and in any environment.

Initial Analysis—The Beginning Point of the HR Program

The basis for an HR program adding value rests on the rationale for its existence and the extent to which it relates to a specific business need. This fundamental concept requires much more attention to the initial analysis that leads to the implementation of an HR program or a continuation of a program. It's the beginning point in the ROI methodology.

The Most Common Reason for Failure

The authors conducted an analysis of almost 500 impact studies involving virtually every type of HR program in a variety of settings, including private and public sector organizations, revealed that the top reason for failure lack of success is the failure to align the program with business or organizational needs from the very beginning.

Although most HR managers are confident in the analysis used to decide if the HR program is needed, in many cases the process is not rigorous enough to make a real connection to the business need. And, if there is no business need in the initial rationale for the program, there is often little or no improvement in the business impact measures, making it impossible to achieve a positive ROI. Therefore, for most organizations a more comprehensive approach (described later) is necessary for the initial analysis leading to HR programs or at least an occasional analysis to see if the program is still necessary. Unfortunately, this initial analysis is often perceived as unnecessary and inappropriate.

The Analysis Dilemma

The upfront analysis for HR problems or issues leading to specific programs and solutions creates a dilemma for the organization. Analysis is often misplaced, misunderstood, and misrepresented. The process conjures up images of complex problems, confusing models, and a plethora of data involving complicated statistical techniques. Analysis is often not pursued to necessary detail for five reasons:

1. *Employee needs and problems appear to point to a solution.* When employee needs and problems are examined, several potential solutions are connected to the needs. The solutions, however, may not be appropriate. If managers are not treating their employees fairly, for example, a training program may not be the answer. Perhaps the managers know how to treat employees fairly and with respect but are not required or encouraged to do so. Consequently, training is not necessarily the appropriate solution.

2. *Solutions appear to be obvious.* Some solutions appear obvious when examining certain types of data. If the base pay of a particular group is lower than a competitor's pay for the same group, the obvious solution to an employee turnover problem is to increase the base pay. Nevertheless, pay is not always the principal reason for departure. Low turnover rates can be achieved in organizations that pay lower-than-average salaries. The cause of the problems must be thoroughly analyzed to ensure that funds flow to the right solution, yielding a positive effect on the problem.

3. *Everyone has an opinion about the cause of problems.* Almost every HR manager who wrestles with HR problems has an opinion about the actual causes of the problem. Other stakeholders may also have opinions about the cause of the problem. Because there are multiple opinions, it is tempting to use the highest-ranking input (usually from the most senior manager) and move forward with a solution. Unfortunately, this practice often leads to allocating resources to an inappropriate solution.

4. *Analysis takes too much time.* Upfront analysis takes time and consumes resources; however, the consequences of no analysis can be more expensive. If solutions are implemented without determining the cause, time, and resources may be wasted and the results can be more damaging than doing nothing at all. If incorrect solutions are

implemented, the consequences can be devastating. When planned properly and pursued professionally, an analysis can be completed within any organization's budget and time constraints. The key is to focus on the right tools for the situation.

5. *Analysis appears confusing.* Determining the causes of problems may appear to be complex and confusing. In reality, analysis need not be very complicated. Simple, straightforward techniques can uncover the causes of many problems and achieve excellent results.

Steps in the Analysis

For many HR programs, the first step in analysis is to examine the actual business need. Too often programs are implemented based on behavioral issues or perception of a problem that may or may not be connected to a business need. Figure 6 shows a needs analysis process that begins with feasibility and develops through preference needs. Figure 7 shows the linkages of the levels between needs analysis and evaluation.

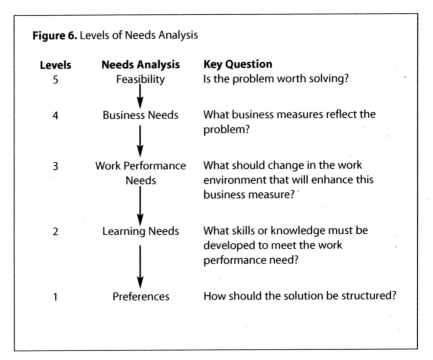

Figure 6. Levels of Needs Analysis

Levels	Needs Analysis	Key Question
5	Feasibility	Is the problem worth solving?
4	Business Needs	What business measures reflect the problem?
3	Work Performance Needs	What should change in the work environment that will enhance this business measure?
2	Learning Needs	What skills or knowledge must be developed to meet the work performance need?
1	Preferences	How should the solution be structured?

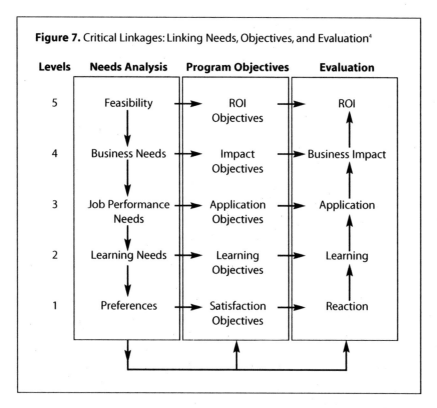

Figure 7. Critical Linkages: Linking Needs, Objectives, and Evaluation[4]

Levels	Needs Analysis	Program Objectives	Evaluation
5	Feasibility	ROI Objectives	ROI
4	Business Needs	Impact Objectives	Business Impact
3	Job Performance Needs	Application Objectives	Application
2	Learning Needs	Learning Objectives	Learning
1	Preferences	Satisfaction Objectives	Reaction

Feasibility

The process begins with initial feasibility issues. The important question here—whether the problem is worth solving—addresses the ROI issue. Is there an expected positive ROI in the solution? Sometimes a problem cannot be solved, or the monetary value of the measure may not move enough to overcome the potential expense of the solution. This initial analysis is crude but examines the overall feasibility of tackling the issue. Because limited resources are available, it is important that detailed analytical skills (and potential solutions) be reserved for issues that really make a difference.

Business Needs

The next step of analysis is the connection to the business need. Is there an actual business measure that is not performing as well as it should? The good news is that there are business measures throughout the organization that reflect HR issues that either need to be addressed or represent opportunities for improvement.

Identifying the business measure(s) is an easy step in the process. Typical business measures include hard data categories of output, quality, costs, and time, as shown in Table 7, and soft data categories of work habits, work climate, job attitudes, customer service, advancement development, and initiative, as shown in Table 8.

Job Performance Needs

The most difficult step in the analysis is establishing work performance needs where the actual cause of the business need improvement is deter-

---

Table 7. Examples of Hard Data[5]

OUTPUT	TIME
Units Produced	Equipment Downtime
Items Assembled	Overtime
Items Sold	On Time Shipments
Forms Processed	Time to Project Completion
Loans Approved	Processing Time
Inventory Turnover	Cycle Time
Patients Visited	Meeting Schedules
Applications Processed	Repair Time
Productivity	Efficiency
Work Backlog	Work Stoppages
Shipments	Order Response Time
New Accounts Opened	Late Reporting
	Lost Time Days

COSTS	QUALITY
Budget Variances	Scrap
Unit Costs	Rejects
Cost By Account	Error Rates
Variable Costs	Rework
Fixed Costs	Shortages
Overhead Costs	Deviation From Standard
Operating Costs	Product Failures
Number of Cost Reductions	Inventory Adjustments
Accident Costs	Percent of Tasks Completed Properly
Sales Expense	Number of Accidents

Table 8. Examples of Soft Data[6]

WORK HABITS	CUSTOMER SATISFACTION
Absenteeism	Churn Rate
Tardiness	Number of Satisfied Customers
Visits to the Dispensary	Customer Satisfaction Index
First Aid Treatments	Customer Loyalty
Violations of Safety Rules	Customer Complaints
Excessive Breaks	

WORK CLIMATE	DEVELOPMENT/ADVANCEMENT
Number of Grievances	Number of Promotions
Number of Discrimination Charges	Number of Pay Increases
Employee Complaints	Number of Training Programs
Job Satisfaction	Attended
Employee Turnover	Requests for Transfer
Litigation	Performance Appraisal Ratings
	Increases in Job Effectiveness

JOB ATTITUDES	INITIATIVE
Job Satisfaction	Implementation of New Ideas
Organizational Commitment	Successful Completion of Projects
Perceptions of Job Responsibilities	Number of Suggestions Imple-
Employee Loyalty	mented
Increased Confidence	Number of Goals

mined. At this level of analysis, the basic issue is to determine what is—or is not—occurring in the job environment that is influencing the business measure in question.

This analysis focuses on the root of the problem or opportunity, detailing what must change to improve the business measure. This is the upfront linkage to the business measure and is the step that is often omitted or it is assumed. This step may involve traditional data collection methods such as questionnaires, surveys, interviews, and focus groups to uncover underlying linkage to business measure improvement. It can also involve brainstorming sessions, problem solving sessions, fishbone diagrams, and other techniques to identify the causes of the problem. This level of analysis may unveil non-HR solutions. Many of the problems that may appear to be HR related may be associated with other issues, such as technology, environment, systems, and processes, which are beyond the influence and control of the HR group. It is important to sort out these causes so that the solution is matched to the actual cause.

Learning Needs

The next level of analysis is the learning gap analysis, which focuses on what individuals need to know to correct the problem. Sometimes the learning gap is the actual solution; the principal business measure problem is that the employees do not know how to do something. When other solutions prevail, the solution usually calls for a knowledge and learning component. For example, if a reward system is implemented, the learning need involves learning how to use the actual reward system and understanding the reward system and processes that make it work successfully. It is a minimal part of the actual solution. Too often learning solutions are implemented when previous analyses were not conducted and it was assumed that learning deficiency was the cause. This disconnect creates tremendous problems because resources are misappropriated and the problem is not addressed. In addition, a negative image of learning is created when it is not needed or misapplied.

Preferences

The final level of analysis is the preference for the solution. In this analysis, HR managers, participants, and other key stakeholders define their preference for the implementation of a particular solution. Preferences may include the location, nature of the delivery, the extent of the implementation, and how and who is involved. Preference needs should be addressed after the solutions are clearly defined. Preferences sometimes shape the actual design and rollout of the solution.

These steps in the analysis are critical but should be applied sparingly. If an HR problem is minor in scope, inexpensive, and not very visible, then it might be better to reduce the analyses to input at the lower levels only. The entire five levels should be reserved for those situations where the projects are strategic, the measure's influence is important to operational issues, the perceived cost of the solution is high, the expected solution is highly visible, perhaps controversial, and the accountability of the solution will attract management's interest. These are almost the identical criteria for considering programs for impact and ROI analysis.

Linkage to Evaluation

Figure 7 shows the linkages of the needs assessment or front-end analysis with evaluation levels. These linkages are critical because they often explain some of important concepts and reveal many of the problems with dysfunctional processes. The objectives of HR programs represent a transition from the needs to evaluation at that same level. This parallel thinking is an excellent way to approach HR needs and programs. It takes

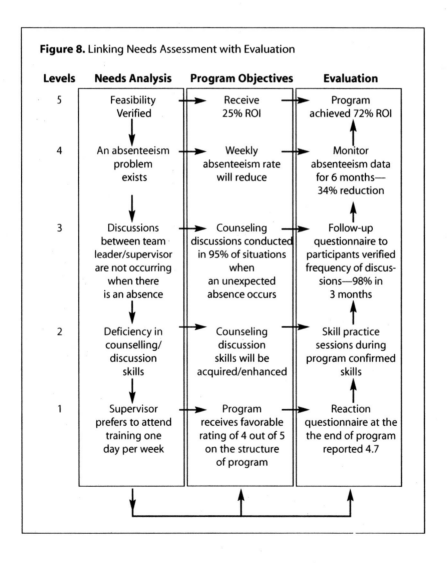

Figure 8. Linking Needs Assessment with Evaluation

Levels	Needs Analysis	Program Objectives	Evaluation
5	Feasibility Verified	Receive 25% ROI	Program achieved 72% ROI
4	An absenteeism problem exists	Weekly absenteeism rate will reduce	Monitor absenteeism data for 6 months— 34% reduction
3	Discussions between team leader/supervisor are not occurring when there is an absence	Counseling discussions conducted in 95% of situations when an unexpected absence occurs	Follow-up questionnaire to participants verified frequency of discus- sions—98% in 3 months
2	Deficiency in counselling/ discussion skills	Counseling discussion skills will be acquired/enhanced	Skill practice sessions during program confirmed skills
1	Supervisor prefers to attend training one day per week	Program receives favorable rating of 4 out of 5 on the structure of program	Reaction questionnaire at the the end of program reported 4.7

a discipline to conduct the analysis at the different levels that lead to the development of objectives at different levels that drive the actual data to be collected at the different levels.

An example underscores the importance of this linkage. A call center was experiencing unusually high absenteeism, which led to an HR solution. Figure 8 shows the analysis that led to the solution. First, the issue of feasibility was addressed. A quick analysis comparing actual absenteeism with benchmarking data and the perceived cost of absenteeism confirmed that is was a problem worth solving.

The business need, the absenteeism rate, was clearly defined and identified. Unplanned, unexpected absences were the key issue, and the absenteeism rate for this category was growing and was higher than other call centers in the same area. The manager of the call center expressed concern that it was too high.

The next level was the determination of the cause of absenteeism. Although there can be many reasons for absenteeism related to the work environment and external issues, in this particular case it was found that the team leaders were not confronting habitual absentees. In essence, the leaders were not conducting counseling discussions when an employee was unexpectedly absent. This discussion, focusing on concern, care, and consequences, is important to change behavior. Absence of discussion is a job performance need. Something is not occurring on the job that should occur, and that is influencing absenteeism. However, it is not necessarily a learning solution unless the team leaders do not know how to conduct these sessions. In this particular case, team leaders did not have the skills to conduct these counseling discussions in a productive way. Therefore, a learning solution emerged to equip team leaders with these counseling skills.

The preference for the solution was defined as two half-day workshops conducted near the job site two weeks apart in which the participants learned how to use the counseling skills and reported progress in the second session.

With a clear needs assessment up front, the objectives were developed and the evaluation data were collected. This approach made the evaluation much easier because the data were clearly defined with the objectives.

The Role of Objectives for HR Programs

The foregoing section presented the linkage between needs assessment and evaluation, with the objectives serving as a transition. The objectives are a critical part of the process and merit further exploration.

Developing Objectives

Ideally, objectives are developed directly from the initial analysis, which identifies the key issues that must be contained in the objectives. The objectives are arranged in a hierarchy, often showing the chain of impact that should be developed after the program is implemented.

Reaction and satisfaction objectives are defined that identify the important issues for acceptance of the HR program. Such measures as usefulness, appropriateness, relevance, importance, and fairness are critical issues that can be explored directly in an objective. The goal is to have an acceptable level of agreement with a particular measure.

Learning objectives are classic in their design. They focus on what skills and knowledge should be acquired as the HR solution is launched. It often follows the process of having a clearly defined statement with a criterion, possibly even with a condition, for example, "Demonstrate the four steps for closing a sale 70% of the time within five minutes."

Application objectives are developed much the same way as learning objectives, but the context is positioned to the job. The application and implementation measure may go beyond typical behavior change and include tasks, steps, processes, and procedures that are either implemented or adjusted. Sometimes a specific criterion is used and the conditions are detailed.

Impact objectives are very measurable and often cover both hard and soft data categories. Hard data categories include output, quality, cost, and time. Soft data categories include such issues as employee satisfaction and customer satisfaction. The measure may be broad, such as, "Increase sales or improve quality," or specific, such as, "Decrease employee turnover from 38% to 25% in six months." The specificity depends on the situation.

ROI objectives are developed when the analysis is conducted at that level. The objective is stated as a desired or acceptable percentage or a BCR. Additional information on establishing ROI objectives is presented in Chapter 6.

Table 9 shows typical objectives at the different levels and specific measures of those objectives. Each of these is taken directly from an HR program. It shows the wide variety of possibilities aimed at the different

Table 9. Examples of Objectives for HR Programs

Objective	Evaluation Level
1. Improve work group productivity by 10%.	Impact
2. Initiate at least three cost-reduction projects in 1 month.	Application
3. Increase the use of counseling discussion skills in 90% of situations where work habits are unacceptable.	Application
4. Achieve a 2:1 benefit-cost ratio 1 year after the new gainsharing program is implemented.	ROI
5. Develop an understanding of the employee assistance program.	Learning
6. Increase external customer satisfaction index by 25% in 3 months.	Impact
7. Handle customer complaints with the five-step process in 95% of complaint situations.	Application
8. Avoid an adverse reaction to the absenteeism control policy.	Reaction
9. Achieve a leadership simulation score average of 75 out of a possible 100.	Learning
10. Conduct a performance review meeting with direct reports within 30 days to establish performance improvement goals.	Application
11. Achieve a 4 out of 5 rating on appropriateness of new ethics policy.	Reaction
12. Decrease the time to recruit new engineers from 35 days to 20 days.	Impact
13. Reduce turnover rate in call centers to 20% annual value.	Impact
14. At least 10% of employees participate in the employee suggestion program.	Application
15. Achieve a positive reaction to flextime work schedule system.	Reaction
16. Involve at least 15% of employees in career enhancement program application.	Application

levels. The challenge is to develop objectives for the program that are as detailed as possible at the highest level possible.

The Power of Higher-Level Objectives

Ideally objectives are established directly from the upfront analysis. When application and impact objectives are developed, much of the design, development, and implementation of the HR program can be influenced by the objectives. For HR program designers, these objectives provide guidance and direction as they develop various scenarios and support tools that will become part of the HR program implementation. For individuals involved in coordinating HR programs, higher-level objectives give them direction so they can relate their own experience or motivation with the desired outcomes. For individuals struggling to make the HR program work, the higher levels of objectives provide them with the specific goals that they often need. Application and impact objectives take the mystery out of the value the program will deliver. Finally, the individuals who sponsor or support the HR programs often find higher-level objectives helpful and essential in describing the impact. They provide more value than traditional reaction and learning objectives.

When Objectives Are Not Available

In some cases objectives are not clearly defined for an HR program, yet the program must be evaluated at the higher levels—impact and ROI. In these cases, objectives must be developed to reflect the actual or perceived impact of the HR program.

This approach involves collecting input from a variety of experts to clearly define the expected outcome of the program, recognizing all of the consequences, both negative and positive. Table 10 shows an example, a contrast between the actual stated objectives from a sexual harassment prevention program and the actual objectives used to capture the value when the program was evaluated. In the initial design, the program was planned to focus on behavior that would ultimately lower the number of complaints. In the revised objectives, some of the outcomes of the program were clearly specified in addition to the sexual harassment complaints. This is a critical issue because many impact studies are conducted for programs that were previously developed but without defined outcomes. This type of program is not necessarily the best candidate for analysis. However, in this case the HR executive continued to show senior executives that this type of prevention program added value to the bottom line. Usually, a level 3 (application) evaluation is appropriate to ensure that the inappropriate behavior has been eliminated.

Table 10. Original and Revised Objectives

Original "Published" Objectives

After participating in this program, participants should be able to:
- Understand the company's policy on sexual harassment
- Identify inappropriate and illegal behavior related to sexual harassment
- Investigate and discuss sexual harassment issues
- Ensure that the workplace is free from sexual harassment
- Reduce the number of sexual harassment complaints

Revised Objectives

Levels	Program Objective(s)
1	Reaction/Satisfaction
	■ Obtain a positive reaction to program and materials
	■ Obtain input for suggestions for improving program
	■ Identify planned actions
2	Learning
	■ Increase knowledge of policy on sexual harassment
	■ Increase knowledge of inappropriate and illegal behavior
	■ Improve skills to investigate and discuss sexual harassment issues
3	Application/Implementation
	■ Administer policy on sexual harassment
	■ Conduct meetings with employees to discuss policy and expected behavior
	■ Ensure that workplace is free of sexual harassment
4	Business Impact
	■ Reduce internal complaints
	■ Reduce external complaints
	■ Reduce absenteeism
	■ Reduce employee turnover
	■ Improve employee satisfaction
5	ROI
	■ Target ROI = 25%

Planning for ROI Projects

HR professionals realize the importance of planning for almost any type of undertaking. Most agree that thorough planning can lead to a more effective implementation. These two issues are understatements when it comes to ROI analysis. Careful planning for ROI analysis saves not only time and effort, but also sometimes makes a difference in the success or failure of the entire project. Planning involves three documents described in detail in this section: the data collection plan, the ROI analysis plan, and the communication and implementation plan.

Data Collection Plan

Figure 9 shows a completed data collection plan for a program designed to prevent sexual harassment. This initial planning document builds on the revised program objectives and defines key issues for data collection. Defining the objectives through the different levels, including ROI, is important. The measures are defined if clarification is needed. This column is particularly relevant for application and impact objectives. For example, a productivity measurement is vague, and, therefore, the definition is critical. The same is true for sexual harassment complaint. Because there are many types of complaints, the definition is important in the evaluation.

The data collection methods are detailed here corresponding to the different levels of objectives using a range of options described in the next chapter. Next, the data sources are identified. In many cases, data are collected from the records in the organization. In other cases, data are collected by the participants involved in the program. In some cases, the managers of participants provide data.

Timing is important to determine specifically when the data are collected from the different sources for each level. During implementation, data often come directly from the participants involved in the solution implementation. In other situations the follow-up can be determined based on when the program is operational and successful.

Finally, the responsibilities are detailed, outlining specifically who will be involved in the data collection.

ROI Analysis Plan

Figure 10 shows the completed ROI analysis plan for the same program. This plan is connected to the previous plan through business impact data.

Figure 9. Sample Data Collection Plan[7]

Data Collection Plan

Program: Preventing Sexual Harassment

Levels	Broad Program Objective(s)	Measures
1	**REACTION/SATISFACTION** Obtain a positive reaction to program and materials Obtain input for suggestions for improving program Identify planned actions	Average rating of at least 4.0 on 5.0 scale on quality, usefulness and achievement of program objectives. 90% submit planned actions
2	**LEARNING** Knowledge of policy on sexual harassment Knowledge of inappropriate and illegal behavior Skills to investigate and discuss sexual harassment	Ability to identify 10 of 10 policy issues From a list of actions, and lack of actions, be able to identify 100% of those that constitute sexual harassment or a hostile environment Demonstrated ability to apply investigative and meditation skills
3	**APPLICATION/ IMPLEMENTATION** Administer policy Conduct meeting with employees Ensure that workplace is free of sexual harassment	Appropriate application of policy Meeting conducted within 30 days Actions taken to eliminate hostile work environment
4	**BUSINESS IMPACT** Reduce internal complaints Reduce external complaints Reduce employee turnover	Decrease formal internal and external complaints related to sexual harassment and a hostile work environment Voluntary turnover
5	**ROI** Target ROI = 25%	Comments: Meet with EEO/AA staff to determine how costs of noncompliance will be identified. Seek management and stakeholder guidance and support to develop a standard monetary value for improvement in employee satisfaction.

Responsibility: _____ **Date:** _____

Data Collection Method/ Instruments	Data Sources	Timing	Responsibilities
Reaction feedback questionnaire	Participant	End of Session	Facilitator
Pre- and posttest Skill practices	Participant	Beginning of session End of session During Session	Facilitator
Self-assessment questionnaire Complete and submit meeting record Employee survey (25% sample)	Participant Workforce	6 months after program 1 month after program 6 months after program	Program Evaluator HRIS Staff Employee Communications
Performance monitoring Self-assessment questionnaire	HR complaint records HR exit records	Monthly for 1 year before and after program 6 months after program	Program Evaluator

Figure 10. Sample ROI Analysis Plan[8]

Program: Preventing Sexual Harassment **Responsibility:** _____ **Date:** _____

Data Items (Usually Level 4)	Methods for Isolating the Effects of the Program/Process	Methods of Converting Data to Monetary Values	Cost Categories	Intangible Benefits	Communication Targets for Final Report	Other Influences/Issues during Application	Comments
Formal Internal Complains of Sexual Harassment	Trend Line Analysis Participant Estimation	Historical Costs with Estimation from EEO/AA Staff	Needs Assessment	Job Satisfaction	All Employees (Condensed Info.)	Several initiatives to reduce turnover implemented during this time period	Complaints of sexual harassment is a significant issue with management
External Complaints of Sexual Harassment	Trend Line Analysis Participant Estimation	Historical Costs with Estimation from EEO/AA Staff	Program Development/ Acquisition	Absenteeism	Senior Executives (Summary of Report with Detailed Backup)	Must not duplicate benefits from both internal and external complaints	
Employee Turnover	Forecasting Using Percent of Turnover Related to Sexual Harassment	External Studies within Industry Evaluation	Coordination/ Facilitation Time	Stress Reduction	All Supervisors and Managers (Brief Report)		
			Program Material	Image of HR	All HR/HRD Staff (Full Report)		
			Food/Refreshments	Recruiting			
			Facilities				
			Participant Salaries and Benefits				

The first column on this plan is the detailed definition of each impact data measure. The next two columns refer to each specific data item.

The second column defines the method for isolating the effects of the HR program on each data item, using one or more of the specific techniques available. The method of converting data to monetary values is listed in the third column, using one or more available techniques.

The next column defines the cost categories for the specific HR program or solution. Using a fully loaded cost profile, all the categories are detailed here. It is helpful to do this during planning to determine if specific cost categories need to be monitored during the HR program implementation.

The next column defines the intangible benefits that may be derived from this program. When listed here, the intangible benefits are only anticipated; they must be measured in some way to determine if they have been influenced by the program. Finally, the other influences or issues that may affect implementation are detailed along with any additional comments.

Communication and Implementation Plan

The communication and implementation plan details how you will communicate data to various groups and how you will monitor and track the results of the evaluation throughout the organization. It also details the specific schedule of events and activities connected to the other planning documents. The targets for communication identify the specific groups that will receive the information. The plan should include the actual method of communicating, the content of the communication, and the timing for the communication, as well.

This plan defines the rationale for communicating with the group and anticipated payoffs, along with the individual responsibility for monitoring actions from the evaluation. This plan clearly delivers the information to the right groups to ensure that action occurs. In almost every impact study, there are significant actions that can be taken.

Resources and Responsibility for Planning

The person responsible for the impact study, usually someone on the HR staff, is generally the one who does the planning. In smaller organizations, the HR manager probably has the responsibility for planning. Planning may take an hour for a simple program evaluation or it may require a full day for more complex programs. Although this seems to be a significant investment in time, it may be the best time spent for the entire project.

Consider planning for ROI early in the process. For programs that are already in operation, planning shows what is involved for collecting, analyzing, and reporting data. For a program that is not yet developed, planning can actually define what would occur in an ideal situation and then drive design and implementation as the program focuses on results.

Final Thoughts

This chapter explored a variety of issues involved in the preparations for ROI. It described in detail when and how you should consider using ROI as a process improvement tool. The initial analysis—the beginning point of the ROI methodology—was explored in terms of what must be accomplished or developed to have a successful ROI evaluation. Objectives, too, are critical to evaluation. This chapter covered how and when objectives are developed and offered several examples of objectives. Finally, the role of planning for an ROI project was presented, detailing all the key steps in the process.

CHAPTER 4

Data Collection Issues

Data collection before, during, and after program implementation is the first but most time-consuming and disruptive step of the ROI methodology. This chapter defines the sources of data and outlines some useful and widely accepted approaches for collecting data.

Sources of Data

The array of possible data sources to provide input on the success of an HR program fall into six general categories. These categories are described in the following sections.

Organizational Performance Records

The most useful and credible data source for impact and ROI analysis is the records and reports of the organization. Whether individualized or group based, these records reflect performance in a work unit, department, division, region, or organization overall. Performance records include all types of measures, which are usually abundant throughout the organization. Collecting data from performance records is preferred for impact and ROI evaluation because these records usually reflect business impact data and are relatively easy to obtain. However, inconsistent and inaccurate recordkeeping may complicate the task of locating performance reports.

HR Program Participants

The most widely used data source for an ROI analysis is participants who are usually the employees directly involved in the HR program. Participants are frequently asked about reaction and satisfaction, extent of learning, and how skills, knowledge, and procedures have been applied on the job. Sometimes they are asked to explain the impact or consequence of those actions. Participants are a rich source of data for evaluation data at the first four levels. Participants are credible because they are the individuals who are involved in the HR program and are expected to make it successful. Also, they are often the most knowledgeable of other factors that may influence results. The challenge is to find an effective, efficient, and consistent way to capture data from this important source. When program participants are represented by a union, it is generally a good idea to seek input from the collective bargaining representative, or at the very least to inform the union that participants will be asked for input.

Participants' Managers

Another important source of data is the individuals who directly supervise or manage program participants. The managers often have a vested interest in the evaluation process because they approve, support, or require the participants to become involved in the program in the first place. In many situations, they observe the participants as they attempt to make the HR program successful by applying their new learning.

Consequently, managers are able to report on the successes linked to the program as well as the difficulties and problems associated with application. Although manager input is usually best for application (level 3) evaluation, it is also sometimes helpful for impact (level 4) evaluation.

Direct Reports

In situations where supervisors and managers are involved in an HR program, their direct reports can be important sources of data. Direct reports can report perceived changes that have occurred since the program was implemented. Input from direct reports is usually appropriate for application (level 3) data. For example, in a 360-degree feedback program, input from direct reports is the most credible source of data for changes in manager behavior and leadership.

Team/Peer Group

Individuals who serve as team members or occupy peer-level positions in the organization are another source of data for some programs. In these situations, peer group members provide input on perceived changes since the program was implemented. This source of data is more appropriate when all team members participate in the program and, consequently, when they report on the collective efforts of the group.

Internal/External Groups

In some situations, internal or external groups, such as the HR staff, program facilitators, expert observers, or external consultants, may provide input on the success of the individuals when they learn and apply the skills and knowledge covered in the program. Sometimes expert observers or assessors may be used to measure learning. This source may be useful for on-the-job application (level 3).

Business Performance Monitoring

One of the more important methods of data collection is monitoring the organization's records. Performance data are available in every organization to report on outputs, quality, costs, time, job satisfaction, and customer satisfaction. In most organizations, performance data are available to measure the improvement resulting from an HR program. If not, additional recordkeeping systems must be developed for measurement and analysis. At this point, the question of economics enters. Is it economical to develop the recordkeeping system necessary to evaluate an HR program? If the cost of gathering or developing the data is greater than the expected value for the entire program, then it is meaningless to develop the systems to capture the data.

Using Current Measures

The recommended approach is to use existing performance measures if available. Performance measures should be reviewed to identify the items related to the proposed program objectives. Sometimes, an organization has several performance measures related to the same objective. For example, a new sales incentive program may be designed to increase sales and the profits from sales, which could be measured in a variety of ways:

- monthly sales per associate;
- average amount of sale;
- average sales per customer;
- number of sales calls;
- close ratio;
- average cost of sale;

- average sales cycle time;
- customer return rate; and
- customer retention rate.

Each of these measures, in its own way, measures the efficiency or effectiveness of the sales team. All related measures should be reviewed to determine those most relevant to the HR program.

Occasionally, existing performance measures are integrated with other data, making it difficult to isolate them from unrelated data. When this occurs, all existing related measures should be extracted and re-tabulated to be compared appropriately in the evaluation. At times, conversion factors may be necessary. For example, the average number of new sales orders per month may be a routine performance measure for the sales department. In addition, the sales cost per sales representative is also reported. However, in the evaluation of an HR program, the average cost per new sale is needed. The two existing performance measures are used when converting sales data to average cost per new sale.

Developing New Measures

In some cases, data are unavailable to measure the effectiveness of an HR program. If economically feasible, the HR staff must work with the participating organization to create systems to develop the measures. Possibly the quality division, the finance department, or information technology section will be instrumental in helping determine if new measures are needed and, if so, how they will be collected. Typical questions to consider when creating new measures include the following:

- Which function will develop the measurement system?
- Who will input the data?
- Where will the data be captured?
- When and how will the data be reported?

In one organization, a new employee orientation system was implemented on a companywide basis. Several measures were planned, including early turnover (the percentage of employees who left the company during the first 6 months of employment), which should be influenced by an improved employee orientation program. At the time of the program's inception, this measure was not available, but when the program was implemented, the organization began to collect early turnover figures for comparison.

Questionnaires and Surveys

Probably the most common method of data collection is the questionnaire. Ranging from short reaction forms to detailed follow-up tools, questionnaires are used to obtain subjective information about participants, as well as objective data to measure business results for ROI analysis. With this versatility and popularity, the questionnaire is the preferred method for capturing the first four levels of data (that is, reaction, learning, application, and business impact).

Surveys represent a specific type of questionnaire with several applications for measuring HR program success. Surveys are used in situations where attitudes, beliefs, and opinions are captured only. A questionnaire has more flexibility and captures data ranging from attitude to specific improvement statistics. The principles of survey construction and design are similar to questionnaire design. The development of both types of instruments is covered in this section.

Types of Questions

In addition to the types of data sought, the types of questions asked distinguish surveys from questionnaires. Surveys can have yes or no responses if absolute agreement or disagreement is required. Alternatively, a response scale, or Likert scale, allows the respondents to select from a range of response points (strongly disagree to strongly agree) on a survey. A questionnaire, on the other hand, may contain any or all of the following types of questions along with Likert-scale-type questions:

- *An open-ended question* has an unlimited answer. The question is followed by an ample blank space for the response.
- *A checklist* provides a list of items where a respondent is asked to check those that apply in the situation.
- *A two-way question* has alternate responses (yes/no) or other possibilities.
- *A multiple-choice question* has several choices and the respondent is asked to select the one most applicable.
- *A ranking scale* requires the respondent to rank a list of items.

Questionnaire design is a straightforward, logical process. There is nothing more confusing, frustrating, and potentially embarrassing than a poorly designed questionnaire. Table 11 shows the steps that help to develop a valid, reliable, and effective instrument.

Table 11. Questionnaire Design Steps

1. Determine the specific information needed

2. Involve management in the process.

3. Select the type(s) of questions.

4. Develop the questions.

5. Check the reading level.

6. Test the questions.

7. Address the anonymity issue.

8. Design for ease of tabulation and analysis.

9. Develop the completed questionnaire and prepare a data summary.

Questionnaire Content

The areas of feedback used on reaction questionnaires depend on the purpose of the evaluation. Some forms are simple, whereas others are detailed and require a considerable amount of time to complete. When a comprehensive evaluation is planned, where impact and ROI are being measured, the reaction questionnaire can be simple, asking only questions that provide pertinent information regarding participant perception. However, when a reaction questionnaire is the only means of gathering evaluation data, then a more comprehensive list of questions is necessary.

Table 12 presents a list of the most common types of feedback solicited. Objective questions covering each of the areas in the table can help ensure thorough feedback from participants. This feedback can be useful in making adjustments in a program, assisting in predicting performance after the program, or both.

In most medium-to-large organizations where there is significant HR activity, reaction instruments are usually automated for computerized scanning and reporting. Some organizations use direct input into a web site to develop not only detailed reports, but also to develop databases, allowing feedback data to be compared to other programs.

Collecting learning data using a questionnaire is also common. Most types of tests, whether formal or informal, are based on questionnaires.

Table 12. Typical Reaction/Satisfaction Questions

- *Progress with objectives:* To what degree were the objectives met?

- *Appropriateness:* Was the program appropriate for the target group?

- *Implementation:* Was the method of implementation appropriate for the objectives?

- *Coordinator:* Was the coordinator effective?

- *Motivation:* Were you motivated to implement this program?

- *Relevance:* Was the program relevant to your needs? The organization's needs?

- *Importance:* How important is this program to your success?

- *Logistics:* Were the scheduling and organizing efficient?

- *Potential barriers:* What potential barriers exist for the implementation of the program?

- *Planned implementation:* Will you implement this program? How?

- *Recommendations for others:* What is the appropriate target group for this program?

- *Overall evaluation:* What is your overall rating of this program?

However, several questions to measure learning can be developed to use with the reaction questionnaire. For example, in the implementation of a new rewards system, it is important to know if the employees involved in the system (the participants) fully understand the rules, procedures, and policies of the new system. Possible areas to explore on a reaction questionnaire, all aimed at measuring learning, are

- understanding;
- knowledge gain;
- skill enhancement;
- ability;
- capability;
- competence; and
- awareness.

Questions to gauge learning are developed using a format similar to the reaction part of the questionnaire. They measure the extent to which learning has taken place, usually based on confidence and perception.

Questionnaires are also commonly used to collect post-program application and impact data. Table 13 presents a list of questionnaire content possibilities for capturing these follow-up data. Reaction and learning data may also be captured in a follow-up questionnaire to compare to similar data gathered immediately after the introduction of the HR program. Most follow-up issues, however, involve application and implementation (level 3) and business impact (level 4).

Table 13. Typical Content Areas for Post-Program Questionnaires

- Progress with objectives
- Use of program materials, guides, and technology
- Application of knowledge/skills
- Change in work or work habits
- Improvements/accomplishments
- Monetary impact of improvements
- Improvements linked to the program
- Confidence level of data supplied
- Perceived value of the investment
- Linkage with output measures
- Barriers to implementation
- Enablers to implementation
- Management support for implementation
- Other benefits
- Other possible solutions
- Target audience recommendations
- Suggestions for improvement

Tests

Testing is important for measuring learning in HR program evaluations. Pre- and post-program comparisons using tests are common. An improvement in test scores shows the change in skill, knowledge, or attitude attributed to the program. You can use performance testing, simulations, role plays, and business games to measure the extent of knowledge or skill increase related to an HR program. Base the design and development of self-assessment questionnaires and surveys on principles similar to those presented in the previous section on questionnaires.

Interviews

Another helpful data collection method is the interview, although it is not used in evaluation as frequently as questionnaires. The HR staff, the participant's immediate manager, or a third party can conduct interviews. Interviews can secure data not available in performance records or data difficult to obtain through written responses or observations. Also, interviews can uncover success stories that can be useful in communicating evaluation results. Participants may be reluctant to describe their results in a questionnaire, although they may be willing to volunteer the information to a skillful interviewer who uses probing techniques. The interview process can uncover reaction, learning, and impact data, but it is primarily used with application data. A major disadvantage of the interview is that it is time consuming and requires interviewer preparation to ensure that the process is consistent.

Interviews fall into two basic types: structured and unstructured. A structured interview is much like a questionnaire. The interviewer asks specific questions that allow the participant little room to deviate from the menu of expected responses. The structured interview offers several advantages over the questionnaire. For example, an interview can ensure that the questionnaire is completed and that the interviewer understands the responses supplied by the participant. The unstructured interview has built-in flexibility to allow the interviewer to probe for additional information. This type of interview uses a few general questions, which can lead into more detailed information as important data are uncovered. The interviewer must be skilled in the probing process. The design issues and steps for interviews are similar to those of the questionnaire. It is important to prepare the interviewer, try out the interview, provide clear instructions to the participant, and follow a plan.

Focus Groups

An extension of the interview, focus groups are particularly helpful when in-depth feedback is needed for evaluation application. The focus group involves a small group discussion conducted by an experienced facilitator. It is designed to solicit qualitative judgments on a planned topic or issue. Group members are all required to provide their input, as individual input builds on group input.

When compared to questionnaires, surveys, tests, or interviews, the focus group strategy has several advantages. The basic premise of using focus groups is that when quality judgments are subjective, several individual judgments are better than one. The group process, whereby participants stimulate ideas in others, is an effective method for generating qualitative data. Focus groups are inexpensive and can be quickly planned and conducted. They should be small (eight to 12 individuals) and should represent a sample of the target population. Facilitators must have the appropriate expertise. This data collection method's flexibility makes it possible to explore a HR program's unexpected outcomes or applications.

Focus groups are particularly helpful when qualitative information is needed about the success of an HR program. For example, focus groups can be used to

- evaluate the reactions to parts or all of an HR program;
- gauge the overall effectiveness of program application; and
- assess the impact of the HR program in a follow-up evaluation after the program is completed.

Essentially, focus groups are helpful when evaluation information is needed but cannot be collected adequately with questionnaires, interviews, or quantitative methods. The focus group is an inexpensive and quick way to determine the strengths and weaknesses of HR programs. For a complete evaluation, focus group information should be combined with data from other instruments.

Observations

Another potentially useful data collection method is observation. The observer may be a member of the HR staff, the participant's immediate manager, a member of a peer group, or an external party. The most common observer, and probably the most practical, is a member of the HR staff.

Observation is often misused or misapplied to evaluation situations, leaving some to abandon the process. Observations should be systematic, minimizing the observer's influence. Observers should be carefully selected, fully prepared, and knowledgeable about how to interpret and report what they observe.

Observation is useful for collecting data on job design issues, compensation, reward systems, compliance, employee training, and performance evaluation. Five methods of observation can be used, depending on the circumstances surrounding the type of information needed. They are listed in Table 14.

Table 14. Observation Methods for Data Collection

Observation Method	Description
Behavior Checklist and Coded Behavior Forms	A behavior checklist is used for recording the presence, absence, frequency, or duration of a participant's behavior as it occurs. Codes are used to abbreviate specific behaviors and steps.
Delayed Report Method	The observer does not use any forms or written materials during the observation and subsequently attempts to reconstruct what has been observed during the observation period.
Video Recording	A videocamera records behavior in every detail.
Audio Monitoring	Conversations of participants, who are using specific skills as part of the HR program, are monitored.
Computer Monitoring	The computer "observes" participants as they perform job tasks.

Improving the Response Rate for Data Collection

One of the greatest challenges in data collection is achieving an acceptable response rate or a certain level of participation. Requiring too much information may result in a suboptimal response rate. The challenge, therefore, is to tackle data collection design and administration so as to achieve maximum response rate. This is a critical issue when the primary data collection method hinges on participant input obtained through questionnaires, surveys, interviews, and focus groups.

The following actions may help boost response rates:

- *Provide advance communication.* If appropriate and feasible, participants should receive advance communications about the requirement to provide data. This step minimizes some of the resistance to the process, provides an opportunity to explain in more detail the circumstances surrounding the evaluation, and positions the follow-up evaluation as an integral part of the HR program, and not just an add-on activity.

- *Communicate the purpose.* Participants should understand the reason for the data, and they should know who or what initiated a specific evaluation. Participants should know if the evaluation is part of a systematic process or if it is a special request for this program.

- *Explain who will see the data.* It is important for participants to know who will see the data and the results of the data collection. If the input is anonymous, the steps that will be taken to ensure anonymity should be communicated clearly to participants. Participants should know if senior executives will see the combined results of the study.

- *Describe the data integration process.* Participants should understand how the results will be combined with other data, if applicable. Participant input may be only one of the data collection methods used. Participants should know how the data are weighted and integrated in the final report.

- *Keep the data collection as simple as possible.* Although a simple instrument does not always provide the full scope of data necessary for an ROI analysis, a simplified approach should always be a goal. When questions are developed and the total scope of data collection is finalized, every effort should be made to keep it as simple and brief as possible. Only ask questions if you intend to do something with the results.

- *Simplify the response process.* Make it easy for the participants to respond. If appropriate, include a self-addressed, postage-paid envelope for mailed surveys and questionnaires. E-mail or web-based questionnaires are preferable in some settings, especially if the questionnaire is being administered at sites in different countries.

- **Use local manager support.** Management involvement at the local level is critical to response rate success. Managers can help with data collection, make reference to data collection in staff meetings, follow up to see if input is provided, and show support for the process.

- **Let the participants know their input is valued.** If appropriate, participants should know that they are part of a carefully selected sample and that their input will be used to make decisions regarding a much larger target audience. This action often appeals to a sense of responsibility for participants to provide usable, accurate data for the instrument.

- **Consider incentives.** At least three types of incentives can be used to boost response rates: (1) **Offer an incentive in exchange for input.** For example, if participants return questionnaires or participate in interviews or focus groups, they will receive a small gift, such as a mouse pad or coffee mug. If identity is an issue, a neutral third party can provide the incentive. (2) **an incentive can be provided to make participants feel guilty if they do not respond.** Examples are a dollar bill (or equivalent currency) clipped to the questionnaire or a pen enclosed in the envelope. Participants are asked to "Take the money, buy a beverage, and fill out the instrument," or to "Please use this pen to complete the instrument." (3) **Obtain a quick response by providing a reward for early responses.** This approach is based on the assumption that quick responses improve response rates. If an individual puts off completing the instrument, the odds of completing it diminish considerably. Those who complete and submit their responses first may receive a more expensive gift or they may be part of a drawing for an incentive. For example, in one study involving 75 participants, the first 25 returned instruments were placed in a drawing for a $500 credit card gift certificate. The next 25 were added to the first 25 for another drawing. After the first 50, there was no incentive. The longer a participant waited, the lower the odds for winning.

- **Have an executive sign the introductory letter.** Participants are always interested in who sent the letter with the request. For maximum effectiveness, a senior executive who is responsible for a major area where the participants work should sign the letter. Employees may be more willing to respond to a senior executive.

- *Use follow-up reminders.* A follow-up reminder should be sent a week after the first request and another reminder one week later. Depending on the instrument and the situation, these times could be adjusted. In some situations, a third follow-up message is recommended. Sometimes the follow-up should be sent via different media. For example, the questionnaire can be sent through regular mail, whereas, the first follow-up reminder is from the immediate manager and a second follow-up reminder is sent by e-mail.

- *Send a copy of the results to the participants.* Even if it is an abbreviated form, participants should see the results of the study. More important, participants should understand that they will receive a copy of the study when they are asked to provide the data. This promise often increases the response rate, as some individuals want to see the results of others along with their input.

- *Review the questions and issues during implementation.* It is critical for participants to understand the planned data collection. It is helpful for them to see an advance copy of the actual data collection plan. Ideally, the instrument should be distributed and reviewed during the session. Each question should be briefly discussed and any issues or concerns about the questions clarified. Ideally, a commitment to provide data is secured from the participant to not only help the response rate, but also to improve the quality and quantity of data.

- *Consider a captive audience.* The best way to have an extremely high response rate is to use a captive audience. In a follow-up session, a routine meeting, or a session designed to collect data, participants meet and provide input, usually during the first few minutes of the meeting. Sometimes a routine meeting (such as a sales, technology, or management meeting) can serve as a good setting to collect the data.

- *Communicate the timing of data flow.* Participants should be provided with specific deadlines for providing the data. They also need to know when they will receive results. The best approach is to determine the last date when the instruments will be accepted, the date when the analysis is complete, the date that they will receive the results of the study, and the date the sponsor will receive the results. A specific timeline builds respect for the entire process.

- *Select appropriate media.* The medium for data collection (whether paper-based, face-to-face, web-based, or e-mail) should match the culture of the group and not necessarily be selected for the convenience of the evaluator. Sometimes an optional response medium is allowed. The important thing is to make the medium fit the audience.

■ *Consider collecting anonymous input.* For surveys and questionnaires, anonymous data is often more objective and sometimes more freely given. If participants believe that their input is anonymous, they are more likely to be constructive and candid in their feedback, and their response rates will generally be higher.

■ *Keep data confidential.* Confidentiality is an important part of the process. A confidentiality statement should be included, indicating that participants' names will not be revealed to anyone other than the data collectors and those involved in analyzing the data. In some cases, it may be appropriate to indicate specifically who will actually see the raw data. Detail the specific steps to be taken to ensure confidentiality. Respondents are told that individual results will not be released and that data will be combined for reporting so that no one person's responses can be singled out.

■ *Conduct pilot testing.* Consider using a pilot test on a sample of the target audience. This is one of the best ways to ensure that data collection is designed properly and that the questions flow logically. Pilot testing the data collection process can be accomplished quickly and effectively with a small sample size. The findings of a pilot test can be very revealing.

■ *Explain how long it will take to provide data.* Although this appears to be a trivial issue, participants need to have a realistic understanding of how long it will take them to provide the data. There is nothing more frustrating to a participant than discovering that an instrument takes much longer to complete than what was estimated. The pilot test should be able to indicate how much time should be allocated for the response.

■ *Personalize the process if possible.* Participants generally respond to personal messages and requests. If possible, the letter accompanying the data collection instrument should be personalized. Also, if it is possible, a personal phone call is a helpful follow-up reminder. The personal touch brings appropriate sincerity and responsibility to the process.

■ *Provide an update.* In some cases it may be appropriate to provide an update on current response rate and the progress on the entire project. It is helpful for individuals to understand how others are doing. Sometimes this communication creates a subtle pressure and reminder to provide data.

Collectively, these items help boost response rates on follow-up data. Using all of these strategies can yield a 60% to 80% response rate for surveys and questionnaires and 90% to 100% for interviews and focus groups, even with lengthy processes that might take 45–60 minutes to complete.

Selecting an Appropriate Method

This chapter presented a variety of methods to capture post-program data for an impact analysis. Collectively, a wide range of methods are available to collect data in a variety of situations. Several issues should be considered when deciding which method is appropriate for a given situation.

Type of Data

Perhaps one of the most important issues to consider when selecting the method is the type of data to be collected. Some methods are more appropriate for impact, but others are better for application. Still others are more appropriate for reaction or learning evaluation.

Table 15 shows the most appropriate type of data for a specific method. Questionnaires and surveys are suited for all levels. Tests are appropriate for level 2 (learning). Questionnaires and surveys are best for level 1 (reaction); although interviews and focus groups can be used for

Table 15. Methods of Collecting Data

	Level 1	Level 2	Level 3	Level 4
Performance Data				✓
Questionnaires/ Surveys	✓	✓	✓	✓
Tests		✓		
Interviews			✓	
Focus Groups			✓	
Observations		✓	✓	

level 1, they often are too costly. Performance monitoring and questionnaires can easily capture level 4 (business impact) data.

Participants' Time for Data Input

Another important factor when selecting the data collection method is the amount of time that participants need to provide their input for data collection. Time requirements should be minimized, and the method should be positioned so that it is a value-added activity (that is, the participants perceive the activity as valuable so they will not resist). This requirement often means that sampling is used to keep the total participant time to a reasonable amount. Some methods, such as business performance monitoring, require no participant time, whereas others, such as focus groups and interviews, require a significant investment in time.

Management's Time for Data Input

The time that a participant's immediate manager must allocate to data collection is another important issue when selecting a data collection method. Always strive to keep the managers' time requirements to a minimum. Some methods, such as focus groups, may require involvement from the manager prior to and after the program. Other methods, such as performance monitoring, may not require any manager time.

Cost of the Method

Cost is always a consideration when selecting a method. Some data collection methods are more expensive than others. For example, interviews and observations are expensive. Questionnaires and performance monitoring are usually inexpensive.

Disruption of Normal Work Activities

Another important issue is the amount of disruption the data collection will generate. Routine work processes should be disrupted as little as possible. Some data collection techniques, such as performance monitoring, require little time or distraction from normal activities. Questionnaires generally do not disrupt the work environment and can often be completed in only a few minutes or even after normal work hours. On the other extreme, some techniques, such as observations and interviews, may be too disruptive for the work unit.

Accuracy of Method

Accuracy is a factor to weigh when selecting a data collection method. "Accuracy" refers to the instrument's ability to correctly capture the data desired, with minimum error. Some data collection methods are more accurate than others. For example, performance monitoring usually is highly accurate whereas a questionnaire is less so. If you need data regarding on-the-job behavior, unobtrusive observation is clearly one of the most accurate processes.

Utility of an Additional Method

Because there are many different methods for collecting data, it is tempting to use too many data collection methods. Using multiple data collection methods adds time and cost to the evaluation and may add little value. Utility refers to the added value of using an additional data collection method. When more than one method is used, the question of utility should always be addressed. Does the value obtained from the additional data warrant the extra time and expense of the method? If the answer is no, the additional method should not be implemented.

Cultural Bias for Data Collection Method

The culture or philosophy of the organization can dictate which data collection methods are used. For example, some organizations are accustomed to using questionnaires and prefer to use them in their culture. Other organizations do not use observation because their culture does not support the potential invasion of privacy associated with it.

Final Thoughts

This chapter has provided an overview of data collection methods that can be used in ROI analysis. Organizations can select from many methods according to their budget or situation. Performance data monitoring and follow-up questionnaires are used to collect data for impact analyses. Other methods can help you develop a complete profile of success of the HR program and its subsequent business impact.

CHAPTER 5

Data Analysis

Data analysis is often the most dreaded part of the ROI methodology. It can also be the most confusing. The goal of this chapter is to explain how you can take the data, isolate the data items that are connected to the HR program, and convert them to monetary values that can be plugged into the ROI formula. This chapter also addresses some of the guiding principles that keep your analysis conservative.

Data Tabulation Issues

As data are collected using one or more of the methods outlined in the previous chapter, several issues need to be addressed and clarified. The first involves the source of the data. The data used in the analysis must be the most credible data available. If data are collected from more than one source, data obtained from the most credible source are used, if there is a distinct difference.

The second issue involves **missing data**. It is rare for all of those involved in an HR program to provide data in a follow-up evaluation. The philosophy outlined in this chapter is to use only available data when tabulating program benefits. In other words, no data means no improvement. This philosophy means that it takes extra effort to collect data from every participant targeted for evaluation. With hard work and discipline, it is possible to achieve participation rates in the 60% to 80% range using appropriate data collection methods.

The third issue relates to **data tabulation and summarization** to prepare it for analysis. Ideally, tabulated data should be organized by evaluation levels and issues. It's possible to develop and analyze tables of data and then include them in the final impact study.

Always review input data to ensure that they are reasonable. The analysis should **exclude extreme data items** and **unsupported claims.**

These principles for initially adjusting, tabulating, and summarizing data are critical to the analysis. They represent a conservative approach and, consequently, can build credibility with the target audience. More on these principles is presented later.

Isolating the Effects of HR

The cause-and-effect relationship between HR and performance data can be confusing and difficult to prove, but it can be demonstrated with an acceptable degree of accuracy. The challenge is to develop one or more specific strategies during data planning to isolate the effects of HR. By addressing the need to isolate the effects of HR right up front, you can ensure that appropriate strategies are used and that costs and time commitments are kept to a minimum.

The Need to Isolate the Effects of HR

Other processes always must work in harmony with HR to improve business results. It is often not an issue of whether HR is part of the mix, but how much is needed and what is the most appropriate implementation needed to drive HR's share of performance improvement.

The isolation issue comes into play when different processes are influencing business results. You need to be able to identify the relative contribution of HR. In many situations, this question has to be addressed: How much of the improvement is attributable to the HR program? Without an answer or a specific method to address the issue, a great deal of credibility is lost, particularly with the senior management team.

The difficulty of isolating HR's effect is often a point of contention. The classic approach is to use control group arrangements in which one group is involved in the HR program and another is not. This technique is the most credible way to isolate the effects of HR. You'll find a more detailed discussion of control groups later in this chapter.

Nevertheless, control groups are not be appropriate for all ROI studies. Consequently, other methods must be used. Researchers sometimes use time-series analysis, also discussed in this chapter as trend-line analysis. Beyond that, many researchers abandon the search, suggesting that the issue cannot be addressed with credibility, or they choose to ignore the issue, hoping that the "oversight" is not noticed by the program sponsor.

Neither of these responses is acceptable to senior manager who are trying to understand the link between HR and business success. A credible estimate often satisfies senior management's requirements. The important point is to *always* address this issue, even if an expert estimate is used with an error adjustment. By so doing, the issue of isolating the effects of HR becomes a routine step in the analysis and builds credibility for the program's influence on key business measures.

Chain of Impact: The Initial Evidence

Before presenting the techniques for isolating HR's impact, it is helpful to examine the chain of impact implied in the various levels of evaluation. As illustrated in Figure 11, the chain of impact must be in place for the HR program to drive business results.

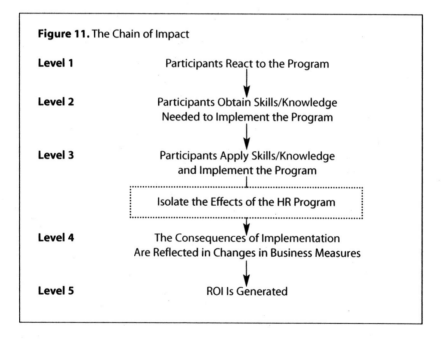

Figure 11. The Chain of Impact

Level 1	Participants React to the Program
Level 2	Participants Obtain Skills/Knowledge Needed to Implement the Program
Level 3	Participants Apply Skills/Knowledge and Implement the Program
	Isolate the Effects of the HR Program
Level 4	The Consequences of Implementation Are Reflected in Changes in Business Measures
Level 5	ROI Is Generated

Measurable business impact achieved through an HR program should be derived from the application of skills/knowledge over a specified period of time after a program has been conducted. Successful application of the HR program should stem from the participants' learning of new skills or acquiring new knowledge in the HR program so they know what, how, and why to do something differently.

Without the preliminary evidence of the chain of impact, it is difficult to isolate the effects of the HR program. Without learning or application, it is virtually impossible to conclude that the HR program caused any business impact improvements. Furthermore, if the program is not viewed as relevant or important, participants are unlikely to make an effort to learn and apply the knowledge or skills.

Developing this chain of impact requires data collection at four levels for an ROI calculation. If you collect data on business results, you should also collect data for the other levels of evaluation to ensure that the HR program has produced the business results.

Identifying Other Factors: A First Step

As a first step in isolating HR's impact on business performance, you should identify all the factors that may have contributed to the performance improvement. The HR program is not the sole source of improvement. Consequently, the credit for improvement must be shared with several possible variables and sources—an approach that is likely to gain the respect of management. Any of several potential sources is likely to reveal information about major influencing factors:

- The sponsors may be able to identify factors that should influence the output measure if they have requested the program.
- The client is usually aware of other programs or solutions that may impact the output.
- Program participants are often aware of other factors that may have caused performance improvement.
- In some situations, participants' immediate managers may be able to identify variables that influence the performance improvement.
- Analysts and program designers may also be able to identify factors that have an impact on results.
- Process owners and other specialists may be able to provide constructive input.
- Finally, middle and top management may be able to identify other influences, based on their experience and knowledge of the situation.

Taking time to focus attention on variables that may have influenced performance brings additional accuracy and credibility to the ROI methodology. Failure to acknowledge that HR programs are but one variable among the many that influence business results can destroy the credibility of an impact report.

Use of Control Groups

The most accurate way to isolate the impact of HR is the use of control groups in an experimental design. This approach involves the use of an experimental group (pilot group) involved in the implementation of an HR program and a control group (comparison group) that is not. The composition of both groups should be as similar as possible, and, if feasible, you should randomly select participants for each group. When this is possible and both groups are subjected to the same environmental influences, the difference in the performance of the two groups can be attributed to the HR program.

As illustrated in Figure 12, the control group and experimental group do not necessarily have pre-program measurements. Measurements are taken after the program is implemented. The difference in the performance of the two groups shows the amount of improvement that is directly related to the HR program.

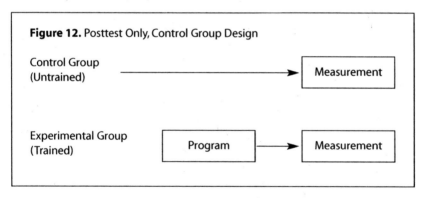

Figure 12. Posttest Only, Control Group Design

Control group arrangements appear in many settings, including both private and public sectors. A turnover reduction program for communication specialists in a government agency used a control group and an experimental group (Phillips and Phillips, 2002a). The experimental group included individuals in a special program designed to allow participants to achieve a master's degree in information science on agency time and at agency expense. The control group was carefully selected to match up with the experimental group in terms of job title, tenure with the agency, and the college degree obtained. The control/experimental group differences were dramatic, showing the impact of the retention program.

One caution to keep in mind is that the use of control groups may create an image that the HR staff is creating a laboratory setting, which can cause a problem for some administrators and executives. To avoid this dilemma, some organizations run a program using pilot participants as the experimental group and do not inform the nonparticipating control group. The control group process does have some inherent problems that may make it difficult to apply in practice. About a third of the more than 100 published studies on the ROI methodology use the control group process. Additional information on control groups is available in other resources (Phillips, Stone, and Phillips, 2001).

Trend Line Analysis and Forecasting

Another useful technique for approximating the impact of HR is trend line analysis. With this approach, a trend line is projected, using previous performance as a base and extending the trend into the future. When the HR program is implemented, actual performance is compared to the projected performance, the trend line.

Improvement in performance over what the trend line predicted can then be reasonably attributed to the HR program if two conditions are met. First, the trend developed prior to the program must be expected to continue if the program had not been implemented. The process owner(s) should be able to provide input to reach this conclusion. Stated otherwise, if the HR program had not been implemented, would this trend continue on the same path established before the HR program? If the answer is no, trend line analysis should not be used. If the answer is yes, the second condition must be considered. This condition requires that no other new variables or influences entered the process after the program was conducted. The key word is "new," realizing that the trend has been established because of the influences already in place and that no additional influences other than the HR program entered the process. If other variables or influences have entered the picture after the program was conducted, another analysis method would have to be used. If both the conditions are met, trend line analysis can be used to develop a reasonable estimate of the impact of the HR program.

Pre-program data must be available before this technique can be used, and the data should have some reasonable degree of stability. If the variance of the data is high, the stability of the trend line becomes an issue. If the data being analyzed address a critical issue and if the stability of the trend line cannot be assessed using a direct plot of the data, more detailed statistical analyses can be used to determine if the data are stable enough to make a projection.

Developing the trend line is quite simple. It can be projected directly from historical data using a simple calculation available in many calculators and software packages, such as Microsoft's Excel spreadsheet program.

The use of trend line analysis becomes dramatic and convincing when a measure moving in an undesirable direction is completely turned around with the implementation of the HR program. For example, Figure 13 shows a trend line of the sexual harassment complaints in a large hospital chain (Phillips and Hill, 2001). As the figure presents, the complaints were increasing in a direction undesired by the organization. A sexual harassment prevention program turned around the situation so that the actual results are in the other direction. The trend line's projected value is significantly higher than the actual results.

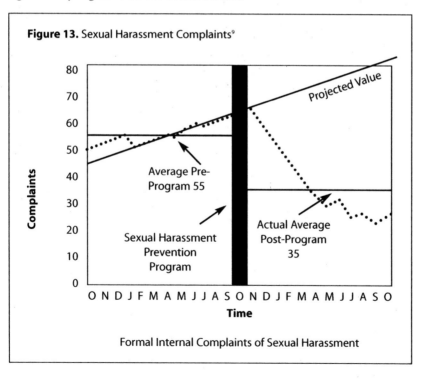

Figure 13. Sexual Harassment Complaints[9]

Formal Internal Complaints of Sexual Harassment

A primary disadvantage of the trend line approach is that it is not always accurate. The use of this approach assumes that the events that influenced the performance variable prior to the HR program are still in place after the program, except for the implementation of the HR program. It also assumes that no new influences entered the situation at the time the HR program was conducted.

The primary advantage of this approach is that it is simple and inexpensive. If historical data are available, a trend line can quickly be drawn and differences estimated. Although not exact, the method does provide a quick assessment of HR's potential impact. About 15% of the more than 100 published studies on the ROI methodology use trend line analysis. If other variables enter the situation, then additional analysis is needed.

A more analytical approach to trend line analysis is the use of forecasting methods that predict a change in performance variables. This approach represents a mathematical interpretation of trend line analysis when other variables entered the situation at the time of the HR program. The basic premise is that the actual performance of a measure related to HR is compared to the forecasted value of that measure. The forecasted value is based on a mathematical relationship with the other influences. The primary advantage of this process is that it can accurately predict business performance measures without the HR program if appropriate data and models are available. Although forecasting is beyond the scope of this book, other references cover the topic (Armstrong, 2001). Approximately 5% of published studies on the ROI methodology use the forecasting technique.

Stakeholder's Estimates of HR's Impact

An easily implemented method to isolate the impact of HR is to obtain information directly from key stakeholders who are usually called the program participants. Participants are the individuals who are primarily involved in the HR program be they non-supervisory employees, managers, or all employees.

For example, when evaluating the effectiveness of a wellness and fitness center, the key stakeholder group consists of the users of the center at all employee levels. These "participants" may be capable of estimating the relative influence of the center on an important measure such as personal health care costs.

The effectiveness of this approach rests on the assumption that participants are capable of determining or estimating how much of an improvement is related to the HR program. Because their actions have produced the improvement, participants may have accurate input on the issue. They should know how much of the change was caused by their actions. Although an estimate, this value typically has credibility with management because participants are at the center of the change or improvement. The estimation approach can be accomplished using a focus group or a questionnaire.

Focus Group Approach. Focus groups work well for this challenge if the group size is relatively small, say, in the range of 8 to12 participants. Larger groups should be divided into multiple groups. Focus groups provide the opportunity for members to share information equally, avoiding domination by any one individual. The process taps the input, creativity, and reactions of the entire group.

The focus group session should take about an hour (slightly more if there are multiple factors affecting the results or there are multiple business measures). The facilitator should be neutral to the process; that is, the same individual conducting the HR program should not conduct the focus group. Focus group facilitation and input must be objective.

The task is to link business results of the HR program to business performance. The group is presented with the improvement in a key business measure. They then provide input as to how much of the improvement is due to the HR program. Table 16 presents the steps to be taken when using focus groups to obtain participant estimates of HR's impact on business performance.

Participants who do not provide information are excluded from the analysis. Table 17 illustrates this approach with an example of one manager's estimations (Phillips and Stone, 2002). The managers were the participants in two HR programs: a change in absenteeism policy (no-fault policy) and a change in the selection process (a screening for previous absenteeism problems).

The manager allocates 50% of the improvement to the policy change. The confidence percentage is a reflection of the error in this estimate. A 100% confidence estimate means certainty, and a 0% confidence estimate means no confidence. A value less than 100% reflects an error in the estimate. In the example, a 70% confidence estimate equates to a potential error range of ±30% (100% - 70% = 30%). The 50% allocation to the policy change could be 30% more (50% + 15% = 65%) or 30% less

Table 16. Steps to Isolate HR Program Effect Using Participants' Estimates

Collecting Participants' Estimates

1. Explain the task to the group members.

2. Discuss the rules.

3. Explain the importance of the process.

4. Start with one measure and show the improvement in the measure.

5. Identify the different factors that have contributed to the improvement.

6. The group identifies other factors that have contributed to the improvement.

7. Start with a factor and discuss the linkage between the factor and the improvement (2 minutes for each member).

8. The process is repeated for each factor.

9. Each member allocates the improvement to each factor (total = 100%)

10. Each member provides a confidence estimate.

11. Members are asked to multiply the two percentages.

12. Results are combined.

Table 17. Example of a Participant's Estimation of Impact

Total Change: 4.2% (8.7–4.5%) Factor that Influenced Improvement	Percentage of Improvement Attributable to the Factor	Confidence Expressed as a Percentage
1. Change in absenteeism policy	50%	70%
2. Change in selection process	10%	80%
3. Increased management attention	10%	50%
4. Unemployment rate	20%	80%
5. Other _____	___%	___%
Total	100%	

(50% - 15% = 35%) or somewhere in between. Thus, the participant's allocation is in the range of 35% to 65%.

In essence, the confidence estimate frames an error range. To be conservative, the lower side of the range is used (35%). This approach is equivalent to multiplying the allocation estimate by the confidence percentage to develop a usable HR program factor value of 35% (50% x 70%). This adjusted percentage is then multiplied by the actual amount of the improvement (post-program minus pre-program value = 4.2%) to isolate the portion attributed to the HR policy. Thus, 1.47% absenteeism rate (4.2% x 35%) is attributed to the new HR policy on absenteeism. The adjusted improvement is now ready for conversion to monetary values and, ultimately, for use in the ROI calculation.

This approach provides a credible way to isolate the effects of HR when other methods do not work. It is often regarded as the low-cost solution to the problem because it takes only a few focus groups and a small amount of time to arrive at this conclusion.

Questionnaire Approach. Sometimes focus groups are not a feasible data collection option. The participants may not be available for a group meeting, or the focus group process becomes too expensive. In these situations, similar information can be captured via questionnaires. Participants consider the same issues as those addressed in the focus group, but, with this approach, the data analysis is based on a series of impact questions embedded in a follow-up questionnaire.

The questionnaire may focus solely on isolating the effects of HR, or it may include a variety of other issues. In some programs, the precise measures that are influenced by the program may not be known. Such is sometimes the case in programs involving diversity, leadership, team building, communications, negotiations, suggestion systems, problem solving, and innovation. In these situations, it is helpful to obtain information from participants on a series of impact questions. These questions show what participants have accomplished and the subsequent impact the program had on the work unit. It is important for participants to know about these questions before they receive the questionnaire. The surprise element can be disastrous for data collection. (This issue will be discussed subsequently.) The recommended series of questions is presented in Table 18.

Collecting an adequate amount of high-quality data from the series of impact questions is the critical challenge with this process. Participants must be primed to provide data; you can do so in several ways.

1. Participants should know in advance that they are expected to provide this type of data along with an explanation of why the data are needed and how they will be used.
2. Ideally, participants should see a copy of the questionnaire and discuss it while they are involved in the HR program. If possible, a verbal commitment to provide data should be obtained at that time.
3. Participants should be reminded of the requirement prior to the time to collect data. The reminder should come from others involved in the process—even the immediate manager.
4. Participants could be provided with examples of how the questionnaire can be completed, using most likely scenarios and typical data.
5. The immediate manager could coach participants through the process.
6. The immediate manager could review and approve the data.

Table 18. Impact and Analysis Questions

1. How have you and your job changed as a result of your involvement in this program?

2. What impact did these changes bring to your work or work unit?

3. How is this impact measured?

4. What is the specific measure (define it)?

5. How much did this measure change with your involvement in the program (monthly, weekly, or daily amount)?

6. What is the monetary value of one unit of this measure?

7. What is the basis for this unit value? Please indicate the assumptions made and the specific calculations you performed to arrive at the value.

8. What is the annual value of this change or improvement in the work unit (for the first year)?

9. Recognizing that many other factors influence results in addition to HR; please identify the other factors that could have contributed to this performance.

10. What percentage of this improvement can be attributed directly to this program (0%–100%)?

11. What confidence do you have in the above estimate and data, expressed as a percentage? (0% = no confidence; 100% = certainty)

12. What other individuals or groups could estimate this percentage or determine the amount?

Several advantages make the questionnaire strategy attractive. It is a simple process that is easily understood by most participants and by others who review evaluation data. It is inexpensive, takes very little time, and requires minimal analysis; therefore, results are an efficient addition to the evaluation process. Estimates originate from a credible source—the very individuals who produced the improvement.

Isolating the effects of HR is not an exact science. Using questionnaires to estimate HR effects is accurate enough for most clients and management groups. The process is appropriate when the participants are managers, supervisors, team leaders, sales associates, engineers, and other professional and technical employees. This technique is the fallback isolation strategy for many types of programs. If nothing else works, you can use this method. Approximately half of the more than 100 published studies on the ROI methodology used questionnaires to isolate the effects of HR.

Using Isolation Techniques

With several techniques available to isolate the impact of the HR program, selecting the most appropriate techniques for the specific program can be difficult. Some techniques are simple and inexpensive, but others are time consuming and costly. When attempting to make a selection decision, several factors should be considered:

- feasibility of the technique;
- accuracy provided with the technique compared to the accuracy needed;
- credibility of the technique with the target audience;
- specific cost to implement the technique;
- the extent to which normal work activities are disrupted by implementing the technique; and
- participant, staff, and management time needed to implement a particular technique.

Consider using multiple techniques or sources for input because two or more sources are usually better than one. Use a conservative method, then, to combine the inputs. A conservative approach builds acceptance. You should always provide the target audience with explanations of the process and the various subjective factors involved. Multiple sources allow an organization to experiment with different techniques and build confidence with a particular technique. For example, if management is concerned about the accuracy of participants' estimates, you could try using a combination of a control group arrangement and participants' estimates to check the accuracy of the estimates.

Converting Data to Monetary Benefits

Traditionally most impact studies stop with a tabulation of business results. In these situations, the program is considered successful if it produced improvements such as productivity increases, absenteeism reductions, or customer satisfaction improvements. Although these results are important, it is more insightful to convert the data to monetary value and show the total impact of the improvement. Also, the monetary value is necessary to compare the cost of the program to develop the ROI. This evaluation is the ultimate level of evaluation, tying HR program results to an impact on the organization's bottom line. This section shows you how leading organizations are moving beyond just tabulating business results and are adding another step of converting data to monetary value.

Sorting out Hard and Soft Data

After collecting performance data, many organizations find it helpful to divide data into hard and soft categories. Hard data are the traditional measures of organizational performance because they are objective, easy to measure, and easy to convert to monetary values. Hard data are often common measures, achieve high credibility with management, and are available in every type of organization. They are destined to be converted to monetary value and included in the ROI formula. Hard data represent the output, quality, cost, and time of work-related processes. Table 7 (in Chapter 3) shows a sampling of typical hard data within these four categories. Almost every department or unit has hard data performance measures available.

Soft data are usually subjective, sometimes difficult to measure, almost always difficult to convert to monetary values, and are behaviorally oriented. When compared to hard data, soft data are usually less credible as a performance measure. Soft data measures may or may not be converted to monetary values. (They may be deemed intangibles.)

Soft data items can be grouped into several categories; Table 8 (in Chapter 3) shows one such grouping. Measures such as employee turnover, absenteeism, and grievances appear as soft data items, not because they are difficult to measure, but because it is sometimes difficult to convert them accurately to monetary values.

A critical point to remember is that you can convert all data to monetary value. Whether the data are considered hard measures or soft measures, you must make some attempt to convert them. You can convert measures of productivity, quality, costs savings, and time savings into cost savings, which is typically considered a measure of efficiency. Revenue, which is already a monetary figure, is converted to profit margin because it is the profit that is intended to improve.

The key to converting data to monetary value is to ensure the credibility of the source of data, the calculations, and the evaluation itself. This section addresses these issues.

General Steps to Convert Data

Before describing the techniques to convert either hard or soft data to monetary values, the general steps used to convert data in each strategy are briefly summarized. These steps should be followed for each data conversion:

1. *Focus on a unit of improvement.* First, a unit of improvement should be identified. For output data, the unit of measure is the item produced, service provided, or sale consummated. Time measures are varied and include such items as the time to complete a project, cycle time, or customer response time. The unit is usually expressed as minutes, hours, or days. Quality is a common measure, and the unit may be one error, reject, defect, or rework item. Soft data measures are varied, and the unit of improvement may include items such as a grievance, an absence, or a change of one point in the customer satisfaction index.

2. *Determine a value for each unit.* A value (V in Table 19, Step 2) is placed on the unit identified in the first step. For measures of production, quality, cost, and time, the process is relatively easy. Most organizations have records or reports reflecting the value of items such as one unit of production or the cost of a defect. Soft data items are more difficult to convert to values, as the cost of one absence, one grievance, or a change of one point in the employee attitude survey is often difficult to pinpoint. The techniques in this section provide an array of possibilities to make this conversion. When more than one

value is available, either the most credible or the lowest (most conservative) value is used.

3. *Calculate the change in performance data.* The change ($\varnothing$ in table 19) in output data is developed after the effects of HR have been isolated from other influences. The change ($\varnothing P$ in table 19, Steps 4 and 5) is the performance improvement, measured as hard or soft data, which is directly attributable to the HR program. The value may represent the performance improvement for an individual, a team, a group, or several groups of participants.

4. *Determine an annual amount for the change.* Annualize the $\varnothing P$ value to develop a total change in the performance data for 1 year. Using a year has become a standard approach to capture the total benefits of an HR program. Although the benefits may not be realized at the same level for an entire year, some programs continue to produce benefits beyond a year. In some cases, the stream of benefits may last several years. However, using 1 year of benefits is considered a conservative approach for short-term solutions. For long-term solutions, a longer, but conservative period is used. The timeframe is established before the study begins.

5. *Calculate the total value of the improvement.* Develop the total value of improvement by multiplying the annual performance change ($\varnothing P$) by the unit value (V) for the complete group in question. For example, if one group of participants for a program is being evaluated, the total value includes total improvement for all participants in the group. This value for annual program benefits is then compared to the cost of the program, usually through the ROI formula presented in Chapter 2.

An example taken from a labor management cooperation program at a manufacturing plant describes the five-step process of converting data to monetary values. This program was developed and implemented after an initial analysis revealed that a lack of cooperation was causing an excessive number of grievances. The actual number of grievances resolved at step two of the grievance process was selected as an output measure. Table 19 shows the steps taken to assign a monetary value to the data arrived at a total program impact of $546,000.

Several techniques are available to convert data to monetary values. Some techniques are appropriate for a specific type of data or data category, and others can be used with virtually any type of data. The HR staff's challenge is to select the particular strategy that best matches the type of data and situation. Each technique is presented next, beginning with the most credible approach.

Using Standard Values

A variety of standard values already exist in most organizations for all types of data including output (profit from shipping one more package), quality (the cost of an error), and time (labor cost per hour). One of the most obvious standard values is time savings from employees. The monetary savings figure is developed by multiplying the hours saved times the labor cost per hour. This time savings value is based on the average salary plus benefits for each individual with a time savings.

The challenge for the HR staff is to locate the standard values, if they exist. Because of Total Quality Management, Six Sigma programs, activity-based costing, and reengineering, many standard values are available in different sections and departments of the organization.

Table 19. An Example to Illustrate Steps to Convert Data to Monetary Values[10]

**Setting: Labor-Management Cooperation Program
in a Manufacturing Plant**

Step 1   *Focus on a Unit of Improvement:*
One grievance reaching step two in the four-step grievance resolution process.

Step 2   *Determine a Value for Each Unit:*
Using internal experts, the labor relations staff, the cost of an average grievance was estimated to be $6,500 when considering time and direct costs. (**V** = $6,500)

Step 3   *Calculate the Change in Performance Data:*
Six months after the program was completed, total grievances per month reaching step two declined by 10. The supervisors attributed seven of the 10 grievance reductions to the HR program by supervisors (isolating the effects of the HR program).

Step 4   *Determine an Annual Amount for the Change:*
Using the 6-month value, 7 per month yields an annual improvement of 84 ($\varnothing$**P** = 84) for the first year.

Step 5   *Calculate the Annual Value of the Improvement:*
Annual value = $\varnothing$**P** x **V**
= 84 x $6,500
= $546,000

Using Historical Costs

Sometimes historical records contain the value of a measure and reflect the cost (or value) of a unit of improvement. This strategy involves identifying the appropriate records and cost statements and tabulating the actual cost components for the item in question.

For example, a large construction firm implemented a program to improve safety performance. The program improved several safety-related performance measures, ranging from Occupational Safety and Health Act (OSHA) fines to total worker compensation costs. Examining the company's records using 1 year of data, the HR staff calculated the average cost for each safety measure (e.g., the cost of an accident).

If all of the costs are available, assigning values based on historical costs is a credible technique. If the time to develop this value is excessive, other methods should be used.

Using Internal and External Experts' Input

When accurate historical records are not available, it might be feasible to consider input from experts. With this approach, internal experts provide the cost (or value) of one unit of improvement. The individuals who have knowledge of the situation and the respect of the management group are often the best prospects for expert input. These experts must understand the processes and be willing to provide estimates and detail the assumptions used in arriving at the estimate. When requesting input from experts, it is best to explain the full scope of what is needed and provide as many specifics as possible. Most experts have their own methodology to develop this value.

When internal experts are not available, external experts are sought. External experts must be selected based on their experience with the unit of measure. Fortunately, many experts are available who work directly with important measures such as creativity, innovation, employee attitudes, customer satisfaction, employee turnover, absenteeism, and grievances. They are often willing to provide estimates of the cost (or value) of these items. Because the credibility of the value is directly related to his or her reputation, the credibility and reputation of the expert are critical.

Sometimes one or more techniques may be used in a complementary way to develop the values. Consider, for example, the process for developing the cost of a sexual harassment complaint filed with the vice president of human resources (Phillips and Hill, 2001a,b). For this analysis, the assumption was made that if no complaints were filed, there would be no costs for sexual harassment activities, including communication, investigation, defense, and settlement.

Consequently, two approaches were used to arrive at the cost of a complaint. First, the direct cost was captured for an entire year of all activities and processes connected with sexual harassment. This figure was taken directly from the cost statements. Second, the other cost values were estimated (e.g., time of the staff and management involved in these activities), using input from internal experts, the Equal Employment Opportunity Commission (EEOC), and affirmative action staff. Figure 14 shows how these two values were combined to yield a total value of $852,000 for 35 complaints, which yielded a value of $24,343 for a complaint.

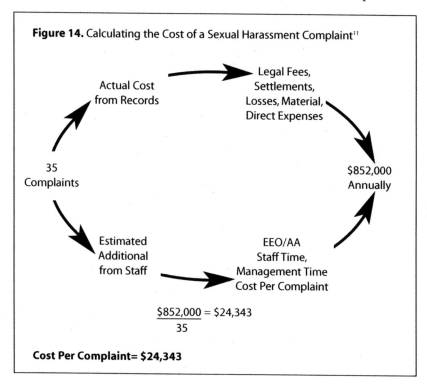

Figure 14. Calculating the Cost of a Sexual Harassment Complaint[11]

Actual Cost from Records

Legal Fees, Settlements, Losses, Material, Direct Expenses

35 Complaints

$852,000 Annually

Estimated Additional from Staff

EEO/AA Staff Time, Management Time Cost Per Complaint

$$\frac{\$852,000}{35} = \$24,343$$

Cost Per Complaint = $24,343

Using Values from External Databases

For some data items, it may be appropriate to use estimates of the cost (or value) of one unit based on the research of others. This strategy taps external databases that contain studies and research projects focusing on the cost of data items. Fortunately, many databases are available that report cost studies of a variety of data items related to HR programs. Data are available on the cost of turnover, absenteeism, grievances, complaints, accidents, and customer satisfaction. The difficulty lies in finding a database with studies or research efforts for a situation similar to the program under evaluation. Ideally, these data come from a similar setting in the same industry; however, this situation is not always possible. Sometimes data on all industries or organizations would be sufficient, perhaps with an adjustment to fit the industry under consideration.

An example illustrates the use of this process. A new program was designed to reduce turnover of branch employees in a regional banking group (Phillips, 2002b). To complete the evaluation and calculate the ROI, the cost of turnover was needed. To develop the turnover value internally, several costs would have to be identified, including the cost of recruiting, employment processing, orientation, training new employees, lost productivity while a new employee is trained, quality problems, scheduling difficulties, and customer satisfaction problems. Additional costs include manager time to work with the turnover issues and, in some cases, exit costs of litigation, severance, and unemployment. Obviously, these costs are significant.

Most HR managers do not have the time to calculate the cost of turnover, particularly when it is needed for a one-time event such as evaluating an HR program. In this example, turnover cost studies in the same industry placed the value at about 1.1 to 1.25 times the average annual salaries of the employees. Most turnover cost studies report the cost of turnover as a multiple of annual base salaries. In this example, management decided to be conservative and adjust the value down to 90% of the average base salary of the employees.

Using Estimates from Stakeholders

In some situations, key stakeholders estimate the value of a soft data improvement. This technique is appropriate when the stakeholders are capable of providing estimates of the cost (or value) of the unit of measure improved through the implementation of the program. When using this approach, participants should be provided with clear instructions, along with examples of the type of information needed. The advantage of this approach is that the individuals closest to the improvement are often capable of providing the most reliable estimates of its value.

An example illustrates this process. The HR department designed a program aimed at lowering the absenteeism rate of the employees in call centers. To calculate the ROI for the program, it was necessary to determine the average value of one unplanned absence. As is the case with most organizations, historical records for the cost of absenteeism were not available. Experts were not available, and external studies were sparse for this particular industry. Consequently, the HR staff asked supervisors to estimate the cost of an absence.

In a group interview format, each participant was asked to recall the last time an employee in his or her work group was unexpectedly absent and describe what was necessary to adjust for the absence. Because the impact of an absence varied considerably from one employee to another within the same work unit, the group listened to all explanations. After discussing the actions taken when an employee is unexpectedly absent, each supervisor was asked to provide an estimate of the average cost of an absence in the company. Although some supervisors were reluctant to provide estimates, with prodding and encouragement most were able to provide a value. The values were averaged for the group, and the result was the cost of an absence to be used in evaluating the program. Although the figure was an estimate, it was probably more accurate than data from external studies, calculations using internal records, or estimates from experts. And, because the estimate came from supervisors who had to confront the issue daily, senior management deemed the estimate to be credible.

In some situations, participants may have difficulty assigning a value to the improvement. Their work may be so far removed from the output of the process that they cannot reliably provide estimates. In such cases, team leaders, supervisors, or managers of participants may be able to provide estimates. In other situations, supervisors are asked to review and approve participants' estimates. In still other situations, senior management provides estimates of the value of data. This approach is used in situations in which it is very difficult to calculate the value or other sources of estimation are unavailable or unreliable.

Linking with Other Measures

When standard values, records, experts, and external studies are unavailable, it is sometimes feasible to examine the relationship between the measure in question and some other measure that can be converted easily to a monetary value. This approach involves identifying existing relationships showing a strong correlation between one measure and another with a standard value.

For example, the classical relationship depicted in Figure 15 shows the correlation between increased job satisfaction and reduced employee turnover. For an HR program designed to improve job satisfaction, a value is needed for changes in the job satisfaction index. In this case, the HR staff was able to determine a correlation between improvements in job satisfaction and reductions in turnover. Using standard values or external studies, the cost of turnover was developed readily, as described earlier. Thus, a change in job satisfaction could be converted to a monetary value or at least an approximate value. There is a potential for error and other factors, but such estimates are often sufficient for converting the data to monetary values.

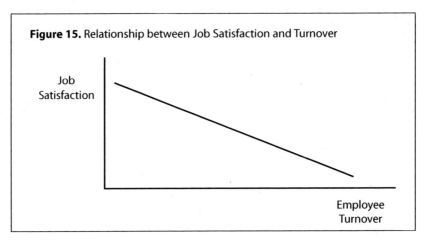

Figure 15. Relationship between Job Satisfaction and Turnover

Selecting Appropriate Techniques: Credibility Is the Key

With several techniques available, the challenge is to select one or more techniques appropriate to the situation. These simple guidelines help determine the proper selection:

- Use the technique appropriate for the type of data.
- Move from most accurate to least accurate techniques.
- Consider availability and convenience when selecting the technique.
- When estimates are sought, use the source with the broadest perspective on the issue.

- Use multiple techniques when feasible.
- Minimize the amount of time required to select and implement the appropriate technique.

All the techniques described here assume that each data item can be converted to a monetary value. Although you can develop estimates using one or more of these techniques, the process of converting data to monetary values can sometimes diminish the estimate's credibility with the target audience who may doubt its use in analysis. Very subjective data—such as a change in employee morale or a reduction in the number of employee conflicts—are difficult to convert to credible monetary values. The question for this determination is this: "Can these results be presented to senior management with confidence?" If the process does not meet this credibility test, you should not attempt to convert the data to monetary values. Instead, list these data as intangible benefits. Other data, particularly hard data items, can be used in the ROI calculation, leaving the very subjective data as intangible improvements.

Other Adjustments

Two potential adjustments should be considered before finalizing the monetary value of an HR program. In some organizations where soft data are converted and values are derived with imprecise methods, senior management is sometimes offered the opportunity to review and approve the data. Because of the subjective nature of this process, management may factor (reduce) the data so that the final results are more credible.

The other adjustment concerns the time value of money. Because an investment in an HR program is made at one time period and the return is realized in a later time period, a few organizations adjust the program benefits to reflect the time value of money using discounted cash flow techniques. The actual monetary benefits of the program are adjusted for this time period. In many situations, the amount of this adjustment is small compared to the typical benefits realized from HR programs. It may be best if you discuss this issue with the chief financial officer (CFO) or the accounting department.

Summary

This chapter identified several issues that collectively not only influence the credibility of an ROI impact study, but also provide a framework from which to develop the ROI report. Therefore, when considering each of the issues, you should consider the following key strategies for developing an ROI impact study and presenting it to the management group:

- Use the most conservative data and assumptions
- Use the most credible and reliable source for estimates.
- Present the material in an unbiased, objective way.
- Be prepared for the potential bias of the audience.
- Fully explain in stepwise fashion the methodology used throughout the process.
- Define the assumptions made in the analysis and compare them to assumptions made in other similar studies.
- Consider factoring or adjusting output values when they appear to be unrealistic.
- Use hard data whenever possible and combine with soft data if available.
- Keep the scope of the analysis very narrow. Conduct the impact study with one or more groups involved in the program, rather than all stakeholders or all employees.

Final Thoughts

Organizations are striving to be more aggressive when connecting HR programs to business results and defining the monetary benefits of HR programs. In this chapter you explored a variety of techniques to isolate the impact of HR programs. It is possible to do so with credibility. Progressive HR managers are taking additional steps to convert business results data to monetary values and compare them with the HR program's cost to develop the ROI. Because an array of techniques is available to convert business results to monetary values, it is possible to identify one or more to fit any situation or program.

CHAPTER 6

HR Costs and ROI

The cost of providing HR programs is on the rise, increasing the pressure for HR managers to know how and why money is spent. Managers need to know the *total* cost of an HR program, which means that the cost profile must go beyond direct costs to include all indirect costs as well. Because you'll be using HR program costs in the ROI formula, it is important to understand cost accumulation and tabulation steps, have an idea of which costs you need to include in your calculations, and know some economical ways to develop cost data.

Cost Issues

Tabulating HR program costs is an essential step in developing the ROI calculation. Fully loaded cost information is needed to manage resources, develop standards, measure efficiencies, and examine alternative delivery processes. The following sections discuss why it's necessary to measure program costs and touch on some important issues around cost data.

Why Measure HR Costs?

Several influences have called attention to the necessity of monitoring HR costs accurately and thoroughly. Every organization should know approximately how much money it is spending on HR. Some HR executives calculate this expenditure and compare it to similar expenditures at other organizations, although such comparisons are unreliable because of the different bases for cost calculations. HR costs as a percentage of operating costs is a standard calculation.

HR staff should know the relative cost effectiveness of programs and their components. Monitoring costs by program allows the staff to determine how costs are changing. If a program's cost rises, it may be appropriate to reevaluate the program's impact and overall success. It may be useful to compare specific components of costs with those of other programs or organizations. Significant differences may signal a problem. Also, costs associated with analysis, design, development, implementation, or operation can be compared with those of other programs within the organization and used to develop cost standards.

Accurate costs are necessary to predict future costs. Historical costs for a program serve as a basis for predicting future costs of a similar program or for budgeting for a program. Sophisticated cost models make it possible to estimate or predict costs with reasonable accuracy.

When an ROI or benefit-cost analysis is needed for a specific program, you'll need to develop cost data. For these analyses, cost data are just as important as the program's economic benefits. Although it is easy to establish direct costs, it is more difficult to determine indirect costs related to a program. To develop a realistic ROI, costs must be accurate and credible. Otherwise, the painstaking attention given to the monetary benefits is wasted because of inadequate or inaccurate costs.

Fully Loaded Costs

The conservative approach to calculating ROI has a direct connection to cost accumulation. HR program costs should be fully loaded for ROI analysis. With this approach, you include all costs that can be identified and linked to a particular program. A fully loaded cost profile includes items such as those in Table 20, below. When you calculate ROI and report to target audiences, the methodology should withstand even the closest scrutiny in terms of its accuracy and credibility. The only way to meet this test is to ensure that you include *all* costs. Of course, from a realistic viewpoint, if the controller or CFO insists on not using certain costs, then it is best to leave them out.

The Danger of Costs without Benefits

Communicating the costs of an HR program without presenting benefits is risky. Unfortunately, many HR managers have fallen into this trap for years. They present costs to management in all types of ingenious ways (for example, cost of the program or cost per employee). Although these costs may be helpful for efficiency comparisons, they can be troublesome without benefits. When most executives review HR program costs, a logical question typically follows: What benefit was received from the program? This is a typical management reaction, particularly when costs are perceived to be high. To avoid this situation, some organizations have developed a policy of not communicating cost data for a specific HR program unless the benefits can be demonstrated or there is a strategy in place to develop the benefits. This approach helps to keep a balance between the two issues.

Cost Guidelines

For some organizations, it may be helpful to detail the philosophy and policy on costs in guidelines for the HR staff or others who monitor and report costs. Cost guidelines detail specifically what costs are included with an HR program and how cost data are collected, analyzed, and reported. Cost guidelines can range from a one-page document to a 50-page manual in a large, complex organization. The simpler approach is better. When developed, the guidelines should be reviewed by the finance and accounting staff. When an ROI is calculated and reported, costs are included in a summary form and the cost guidelines are referenced in a footnote or attached as an appendix.

Cost Monitoring Issues

The HR staff has at its disposal several approaches to monitor costs associated with HR programs. The following sections outline several such methods.

HR Program Steps and Costs

One way to consider HR program costs is within the framework of how the HR program unfolds. Figure 16 shows the HR program implementation cycle, beginning with initial analysis and progressing to evaluation and reporting of the results. These functional process steps represent the typical flow of work.

To address an HR need, the organization develops or acquires a solution and then implements it. The HR staff routinely reports to the client or sponsor throughout the process and then undertakes an evaluation to show the project's success. There is also a group of costs to support the process, for example, administrative support and overhead costs. To fully understand costs, the project should be analyzed in these different categories, as described later in this chapter.

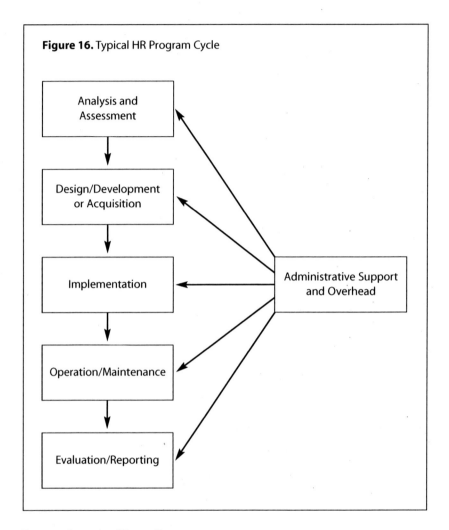

Figure 16. Typical HR Program Cycle

Prorated versus Direct Costs

Usually all cost data related to an HR program are collected and expensed to that program. However, you'll find that some cost categories should be prorated. For example, initial analysis, design and development, and acquisition are significant costs that should be prorated over the life of the program. Using a conservative approach, the life of the program is usually considered to be short term. Some organizations consider one year of operation for the program; others may consider two or three years. For major HR technology investments, the life could be up to five years. If there is some dispute about the specific time period to be used in the pro-rating formula, the shorter period should be used. If possible, consult with finance and accounting staff to help you arrive at prorated costs.

Consider, for example, the cost of developing a knowledge exchange program for a large consulting organization. In this web site, consultants are encouraged to enter and retrieve data about knowledge, capability, and experience. The system was designed to save time and costs with proposals and consulting projects as consultants used the web site. The cost of the software and programming was prorated over the expected life of the project, which was estimated to be five years. An ROI evaluation was undertaken based on benefits for one year. Therefore, to arrive at an annual ROI, the HR staff used one-fifth of the development costs in the analysis.

Employee Benefits Factor

The ROI analysis should include salaries for the time spent by stakeholders and HR staff associated with HR programs, as well as the cost of their benefits over that time. Employee benefits are expressed as a percentage of payroll (salaries). Organizations usually have this figure readily available for use in a variety of cost applications. It represents the cost of all employee benefits expressed as a percent of base salaries. In some organizations this value is as high as 50% or 60%. In others, it may be as low as 25% or 30%. The average in the United States is approximately 38% (U.S. Chamber of Commerce, 2003).

Major Cost Categories

The most important task is to define which specific costs are included in a tabulation of HR program costs. This task involves decisions that will be made by the HR staff and, in most cases, approved by management. If appropriate, finance and accounting staff may need to approve the list. Table 20 shows the recommended cost categories for a fully loaded, conservative approach to estimating costs. Each category is described below.

Initial Assessment and Analysis

One of the most overlooked cost items is the cost of conducting the initial assessment of the need for the HR program. In some programs this cost is zero because the program is implemented without an initial assess-

Table 20. HR Program Cost Categories[12]

Cost Item	Prorated	Expensed
Initial Assessment and Analysis	✓	
Design and Development	✓	
Acquisition	✓	
Implementation		✓
■ Salaries/Benefits—Coordination		✓
■ Materials and Supplies		✓
■ Travel		✓
■ Facilities		✓
■ Participants' Salaries/Benefits		✓
Operation and Maintenance		✓
Evaluation		✓
Overhead/Human Resources	✓	

ment of need. However, as organizations focus increased attention on needs assessment, this item will become a more significant cost in the future.

You should attempt to collect data on all costs associated with the assessment and analysis to the fullest extent possible. These costs include the time of staff members conducting the assessment, direct fees, and expenses for external consultants who conduct the needs assessment, and internal services and supplies used in the analysis. The total costs are usually prorated over the life of the program. Depending on the type and nature of the program, the life cycle should be kept to a reasonable number in the one- to two-year timeframe. The exception would be expensive programs for which the needs are not expected to change significantly for several years.

Design and Development Costs

One of the most significant items is the cost of designing and developing the HR program. This cost item includes internal staff and consultant time for both design and development of software, CD-ROMs, and other support material directly related to the program. As with needs assessment costs, design and development costs are usually prorated, perhaps by using the same timeframe. One to two years is recommended unless the program is expected to remain unchanged for many years and the design/development costs are significant.

Acquisition Costs

In lieu of development costs, many organizations purchase HR programs to use off-the-shelf or in a modified format. The acquisition costs for these programs include the purchase price and other costs associated with the rights to implement the program. These acquisition costs should be pro-rated usually over one or two years using the same rationale described above. If the organization needs to modify or further develop the program, these costs should be included as development costs. In practice, many programs have both acquisition costs and development costs.

Implementation Costs

An important segment of HR program costs is the implementation costs. Five major categories are included:

1. *Salaries of coordinators and organizers:* The salaries of all individuals involved in coordination should be included. If a coordinator is involved in more than one program, the time should be allocated to the specific program under review. The important issue is to account for all the direct time of internal employees or external consultants who work with the program. Include the employee benefits factor each time direct labor costs are involved.

2. *Materials and supplies:* Specific program materials such as brochures, guides, job aids, and CD-ROMs should be included in the delivery costs, along with license fees, user fees, and royalty payments.

3. *Travel expenses:* Include direct costs of travel, if required, for stakeholders, facilitators, or coordinators. Lodging, meals, and other expenses also fall under this category.

4. *Facilities for meetings:* Take into account the direct cost of the meeting facilities. When external meetings are held, this item represents the direct charge from the conference center or hotel. If meetings are held internally, use of the meeting room represents a cost to the organization and should be included even if it is not the practice to include facility costs in other reports.

5. *Stakeholders' salaries and benefits:* The salaries plus employee benefits of stakeholders for their time away from work represent an expense that should be included. Estimates are appropriate in the analysis.

Operation and Maintenance

Under this item, you should include all costs related to routine operation of the program. This category encompasses all costs in the same categories listed under implementation, plus equipment and services.

Evaluation

The total evaluation cost is included in the program costs to compute the fully loaded cost. For ROI evaluation, you should incorporate the costs of developing the evaluation strategy and plans, designing instruments, collecting data, analyzing data, and preparing and distributing reports. Cost categories include time, purchased services, materials, purchased instruments, and surveys.

Overhead/Human Resources

A final charge is the cost of overhead—the additional costs in the HR function not directly related to a particular HR program. The overhead category represents any HR department cost not considered in the above calculations. Typical items include the cost of administrative support, administrative expenses, salaries of HR managers, and other fixed costs. A rough estimate developed through some type of allocation plan is usually sufficient.

Cost Reporting

Here you'll have a chance to follow an actual case study that demonstrates how to present total costs. Table 21 shows the cost for a major executive leadership program (Phillips, 2001). This was an extensive leadership program involving four off-site, weeklong training sessions with personal coaches and learning coaches assigned to the participants. Working in teams, participants tackled a project that was important to top executives. Each team reported the results to management. The project teams could hire consultants as well. These costs are listed as project costs. The costs for the first group of 22 participants are detailed in Table 21.

The issue of prorating costs was an important consideration. In this case, it was reasonably certain that a second group would be conducted. The analysis, design, and development expenses of $580,657 could, therefore, be prorated over two sessions. Consequently, in the actual ROI calculation, half of this number was used to arrive at the total value

Table 21. Leadership Development Program Costs[13]

PROGRAM COSTS

Analysis/Design/Development

External Consultants	$ 525,330
Leadership Center	28,785
Management Committee	26,542

Implementation and Operation

Conference Facilities (Hotel)	142,554
Consultants/External	812,110
Leadership Center Salaries and Benefits (for direct work with the program)	15,283
Leadership Center Travel Expenses	37,500
Management Committee (time)	75,470
Project Costs ($25,000 x 4)	100,000
Participant Salaries and Benefits (class sessions) (Average daily salary x benefits factor x number of program days)	84,564
Participant Salaries and Benefits (project work)	117,353
Travel & Lodging for Participants	100,938
Cost of Materials (handouts, purchased materials)	6,872

Research and Evaluation

Research	110,750
Evaluation	125,875
Total Costs	$2,309,926

($290,328). This left a total program cost of $2,019,598 to include in the analysis ($2,309,926 - $290,328). On a participant basis, this was $91,800, or $22,950 for each week of formal sessions. Although this program was expensive, it was still close to benchmark data of weekly costs for several senior executive leadership programs involving the same time commitments.

ROI: Basic Issues

Now, you'll have a chance to develop a sound base for performing ROI analyses. The following sections cover some fundamental terminology, use of annualized values, and methods for calculating BCRs and ROI.

Definition

The term "return on investment" is often misused. Sometimes it is used in a broad sense to include any benefit from the HR program, a vague concept in which even subjective data linked to a program are included in the concept of the return. In this book, "return on investment" has a precise meaning; it represents a value developed by comparing program benefits to costs. The two most common measures are the BCR and the ROI formulas. Both are presented along with other approaches that calculate the return.

Annualized Values

The formulas presented in this chapter use annualized values so that the first-year impact of the program investment is developed. Using annual values is a generally accepted practice for developing the ROI. This approach is a conservative way to develop the ROI because many short-term HR programs have added value in the second or third year of operation. For long-term HR programs, longer timeframes are used. For example, in an ROI analysis of a self-directed team project, Litton Industries used a seven-year timeframe in the analysis. However, for many HR programs, first-year values are appropriate.

Benefit-Cost Ratio

One of the first methods used for evaluating HR investments is the BCR. As you may recall from Chapter 2, this method compares the benefits of the program to the costs in a ratio. In formula form, the ratio is:

$$\text{Benefit-Cost Ratio (BCR)} = \frac{\text{HR Program Benefits}}{\text{HR Program Costs}}$$

In simple terms, the BCR compares the annual economic benefits of the program to the cost of the program. A BCR of 1 means that the benefits equal the costs. A BCR of 2, usually written as 2:1, indicates that for $1 spent on the program, $2 was returned as benefits. Some HR executives prefer to use the BCR instead of ROI.

ROI Formula

Perhaps the most appropriate formula for evaluating HR investments is *net* program benefits divided by costs. The ratio is usually expressed as a percentage. In formula form, the ROI becomes:

$$\text{ROI (\%)} = \frac{\text{HR Program Benefits - HR Program Costs}}{\text{HR Program Costs}} \times 100$$

or

$$\text{ROI (\%)} = \frac{\text{HR Program Net Benefits}}{\text{HR Program Costs}} \times 100$$

You can derive the ROI value from the BCR subtracting 1 and then multiplying by 100. For example, a BCR of 2.45 is the same as an ROI value of 145%:

$$2.45 - 1 = 1.45$$

$$1.45 \times 100 = 145\% \text{ ROI.}$$

This formula is essentially the same as ROI in other types of investments. For example, when a firm builds a new plant, the ROI is calculated by dividing annual earnings by the investment. The annual earnings figure is comparable to net benefits (annual benefits minus the cost). The investment is comparable to program costs, which represent the investment in the program.

Using the ROI formula essentially places HR investments on a level playing field with other investments by using the same formula and similar concepts. The ROI calculation is easily understood by key management and financial executives who regularly use ROI with other investments.

The following example illustrates the use of the BCR and ROI. A large metropolitan bus system introduced a new program to reduce unscheduled absences (Phillips and Stone, 2002). The increase in absences left the system facing many delays, forcing the system to create a large pool of drivers to fill in for the absent drivers. The pool had become substantial, representing a significant expenditure. The program involved a change in policy and a change in the selection process, coupled with meetings and communication.

The result of the HR programs was some significant improvements, as demonstrated when the program's benefits were compared to its costs in a one-year follow-up. The first year's payoff was $662,000, based on the two major interventions: a no-fault policy and modifications to the screening process. The total, fully loaded implementation cost was $67,400. Therefore, the BCR was:

$$BCR = \frac{\$662,000}{\$67,400} = 9.82$$

Therefore, for every dollar invested in this program, almost $10 in benefits was returned. The ROI was:

$$ROI = \frac{\$662,000 - 67,400}{\$67,400} \times 100 = 882\%$$

For every $1 invested in the program, the costs (investment) were recovered, and an additional $8.82 dollars were "returned" as earnings.

ROI Interpretation

Choosing the Right Formula

Which quantitative measure best represents top management goals? Many managers are preoccupied with the measures of sales, profits (net income), and profit percentages (the ratio of profits to dollar sales). However, the ultimate test of profitability is not the absolute amount of profit or the relationship of profit to sales. The critical test is the relationship of profit to invested capital, and the most popular way of expressing this relationship is by means of ROI (Anthony and Reece, 1983).

Profits can be generated through increased sales or cost savings. In practice, there are more opportunities for cost savings than there are for profit. Cost savings can be generated when there is improvement in productivity, quality, efficiency, cycle time, or actual cost reduction. A review of almost 500 studies in which the authors have been involved showed that cost savings was the basis for profits in the vast majority. Approximately 85% of the studies had payoffs based on output, quality, efficiency, time, or cost reduction. The others had payoffs based on sales increases, where the earnings derived from the profit margin. This issue is important for nonprofit and public organizations for which the profit opportunity is often unavailable. Most HR initiatives are connected directly to the cost savings portion; therefore, ROI calculations can still be developed in those settings.

The finance and accounting literature define ROI as net income (earnings) divided by investment. In the context of HR programs, net income is equivalent to net monetary benefits (program benefits minus program costs). Investment is equivalent to program costs. The term *investment* is used in three different senses in financial analysis, thus giving three different ROI ratios: return on assets (ROA), return on owners' equity (ROE), and return on capital employed (ROCE).

Financial executives have used the ROI approach for centuries. Still, this technique did not become widespread in industry for evaluating operating performance until the early 20th century. Conceptually, ROI has innate appeal because it blends all the major ingredients of profitability in one number; the ROI statistic by itself can be compared with opportunities elsewhere (both inside and outside). Practically, however, ROI is an imperfect measurement that should be used in conjunction with other performance measurements (Horngren, 1982).

It is important for the formula defined above to be used. Deviations from the formula can create confusion not only among users, but also among the finance and accounting staff. The CFO and the finance and accounting staff should be partners in the implementation of the ROI methodology. Without their support, involvement, and commitment, it is difficult to use ROI on a wide-scale basis. It is important for HR staff use the same financial terms and in the same way as the CFO, as well as the finance and accounting staff, do.

Table 22 shows how some have misused financial terms in the literature. Terms such as "return on intelligence" (or information) abbreviated as ROI confuse the CFO who is thinking that ROI is the actual return on investment. Sometimes "return on expectations" (ROE), "return on anticipation" (ROA), or "return on client expectations" (ROCE) are used, confusing the CFO who is thinking of return on equity, return on assets, and return on capital employed, respectively. Using such terms in the calculation of a payoff of HR investment does nothing except perhaps to confuse and diminish the support of the finance and accounting staff.

Other terms, such as "return on people," "return on resources," "human capital value," and "return on web," are used with almost no consistent financial calculations. The bottom line: Don't confuse the CFO. Consider him or her to be your ally, and use the same terminology, processes, and concepts when applying financial returns for programs.

ROI Objectives: The Ultimate Challenge

When reviewing the specific ROI calculation and formula, it is helpful to

Table 22. Misuse of Financial Terms

TERM	MISUSE	CFO DEFINITION
ROI	Return of Information or Return on Intelligence	Return on Investment
ROE	Return on Expectation	Return on Equity
ROA	Return on Anticipation	Return on Assets
ROCE	Return on Client Expectation	Return on Capital Employed
ROP	Return on People	?
ROR	Return on Resources	?
HCV	Human Capital Value	?
ROW	Return on Web	?

position the ROI calculation in the context of all the data. The ROI calculation is only one measure generated with the ROI methodology. Six types of data are developed, five of which are the five levels of evaluation. A specific objective drives the data collection for each level of evaluation, as described earlier. In terms of ROI, specific objectives are often set, creating the expectations of an acceptable ROI calculation. Table 23 shows the benefits of a sexual harassment prevention program and links the results at the different levels to the specific objectives of the program (Phillips and Hill, 2001b).

As you establish objectives, collect data to indicate the extent to which that particular objective was met. This is the ideal framework to show clearly the powerful connection between objectives and measurement and evaluation data. The table also shows the chain of impact as reaction leads to learning, which leads to application, which leads to business impact and to ROI. The intangible data shown in the business impact category are items that are purposely not converted to monetary value. Intangible measures could have been anticipated in the project before it was implemented. Other measures may not be have been anticipated but were described as a benefit by those involved in the program.

In this particular example, there was an expectation of 25% for ROI (the ROI objective). This organization uses 25% as a standard for all its ROI projects. It is important to note in this example that the ROI objective was not the motivation to pursue the project. The goal was to remove the potential illegal or unethical behavior. Nevertheless, the HR executive wanted to show the senior executives the preventive programs could add value beyond the cost of the program. Because of the sensitivity of the ROI data in this example, the HR executive did not distribute the information to a general audience. Rather, implementation and impact data were presented.

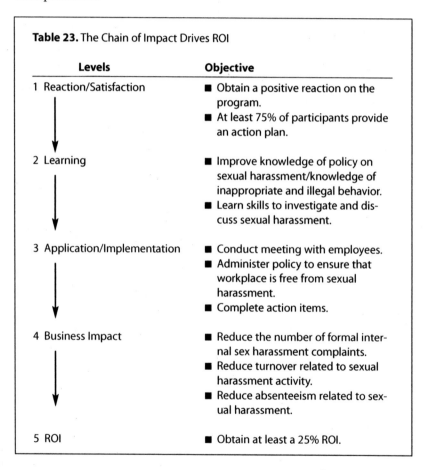

Table 23. The Chain of Impact Drives ROI

Levels	Objective
1 Reaction/Satisfaction	■ Obtain a positive reaction on the program. ■ At least 75% of participants provide an action plan.
2 Learning	■ Improve knowledge of policy on sexual harassment/knowledge of inappropriate and illegal behavior. ■ Learn skills to investigate and discuss sexual harassment.
3 Application/Implementation	■ Conduct meeting with employees. ■ Administer policy to ensure that workplace is free from sexual harassment. ■ Complete action items.
4 Business Impact	■ Reduce the number of formal internal sex harassment complaints. ■ Reduce turnover related to sexual harassment activity. ■ Reduce absenteeism related to sexual harassment.
5 ROI	■ Obtain at least a 25% ROI.

ROI Targets

Specific expectations for ROI should be developed before undertaking an evaluation study. Although there are no generally accepted standards, four strategies have been used to establish a minimum expected requirement, or hurdle rate, for ROI in an HR program. The first approach is to **set the ROI using the same values used to invest in capital expenditures,** such as equipment, facilities, and new companies. For North America, Western Europe, and most of the Asian Pacific area, including Australia and New Zealand, the cost of capital has been reasonable and this internal hurdle rate for ROI is usually in the range of 15% to 20%. By using this strategy, HR executives would set the ROI target the same as the value expected from other investments.

A second strategy is to **use an ROI target that represents a higher standard than the value required for other investments.** This target value is above the percentage required for other types of investments. The rationale: ROI application in HR is still relatively new and often involves subjective input, including estimates. Because of that, it is appropriate to apply a higher standard. For most organizations in North America, Western Europe, and the Asian Pacific area, this value is usually set at 25%.

A third strategy is to **set the ROI target at the breakeven point** (0% ROI), which is equivalent to a BCR of 1. The rationale for this approach is an eagerness to recapture the cost of the HR program only. This is the ROI objective for many public sector organizations. If the funds expended for programs can be captured, there is still value and benefit from the program through the intangible measures, which are not converted to monetary values and the behavior change that is evident in the application and implementation data.

Finally, a fourth, and sometimes recommended, strategy is to **let the client or program sponsor set the ROI target.** In this scenario, the individual who initiates, approves, sponsors, or supports the program, establishes the ROI objective. Almost every program has a major sponsor and that person may be willing to offer the acceptable value. If so, this input links the expectations of financial return directly to the expectations of the individual sponsoring the HR program.

ROI Can Be Very High

As the examples in this book have demonstrated, the actual ROI value can be quite high—far exceeding what might be expected from other types of investments in plant, equipment, and other companies. It is not unusual for programs involved in leadership, innovation, retention improvement, productivity improvement, cost reduction, and reward systems to generate ROIs in the 100% to 700% range. This does not mean that all ROI studies are positive; many are, in fact, negative. Nevertheless, the impact of some HR programs can be quite impressive when a specific need has been identified and a performance gap exists, the HR program is implemented at the right time at a reasonable cost, the program is implemented and supported in the work setting, and the program is linked to one or more business measures. When these conditions are met, it is possible to achieve high ROI values.

It is helpful to remember what drives the ROI value. Consider, for example, the investment in team leaders to reduce turnover. If a leader's behavior changes as he or she works directly with the team, a chain of impact can produce a measurable change in performance from the team. This measure now represents the team's measure of turnover. That behavior change, translated into a measured improvement for the entire year, can be quite significant. When the monetary value of the team's turnover improvement is considered for an entire year and compared to the relatively small amount of investment in one team leader, it is easy to see why this number can be quite large.

What Happens When the ROI Is Negative?

Perhaps one of the greatest fears of the program sponsor or owner and those who are involved in the design, development, and implementation of the program is the possibility of having a negative ROI value. Few individuals want to be involved in a process that exposes a failure, especially their own. They may be concerned that the failure reflects unfavorably on them.

Ironically, a negative ROI study provides the best opportunity to learn and improve processes. The ROI methodology reveals problems and barriers. As data are collected through the chain of impact, the reasons for failure become clear. Data on barriers and enablers generated during application and implementation usually reveal why the program was not successful. Although a negative ROI study is the ultimate learning opportunity, no one wants to invite the opportunity to his or her back door. The preference would be to learn from others.

Sometimes the damage created by a negative ROI stems from expectations that are not managed properly up front and the fear of the consequences of a negative ROI. You can apply the following strategies to help minimize the unfavorable and sometimes disastrous perceptions of a negative ROI:

1. *Raise questions about the feasibility of the impact study.* Is it appropriate to use the ROI methodology for this particular program? Sometimes, a program, by its very nature, may appear to be a failure, at least in terms of ROI, but it succeeds in some other important way.

2. *Make sure there is a clear understanding of the consequences of a negative ROI.* This issue should be addressed early and often. The ROI methodology is a process improvement tool and not a performance evaluation tool for the HR staff. The individuals involved should not necessarily be penalized or have their performance evaluated unfavorably because of the negative ROI.

3. *Look for warning signs early in the process.* Warning signs are usually everywhere. Reaction data can often send strong signals that an evaluation may result in a negative ROI. Perhaps the participants see no relevance of the program or decline the opportunity to implement it.

4. *Manage expectations.* It is best to lower expectations around ROI. Anticipating a high ROI value and communicating it to the client or other stakeholders can create an expectation that will not materialize. Keep the expectations low and the delivery high.

5. *Reposition the story using the negative data.* Instead of communicating that great results have been achieved with this effective program, the story now becomes, "We have excellent information that tells how to change the program to improve results." This is more than a play on words; it underscores the importance of understanding what went wrong and what can be done in the future.

6. *Use the information to drive change.* Sometimes the negative ROI can be transformed into a positive ROI with some minor alterations of the program. You may need to address implementation issues in terms of support, responsibility, and involvement. In other situations, a complete redesign of the program may be necessary. In a few isolated cases, discontinuing the program may be the only option. Whatever the option, use the data to drive action so that maximum value of conducting the study can been realized.

Consequences of Not Implementing an HR Program

For some organizations, the consequences of not providing an HR program can be quite serious. An organization's inability to perform adequately might mean that it is unable to take on additional projects or that it may lose existing projects because of major problems. HR can also help avoid serious operational problems (absenteeism), noncompliance issues (EEO violations), or retention problems (employee turnover rate). In such situation, the method of calculating the ROI is the same and involves these steps:

- Recognize that there is a potential problem, loss, or negative consequence if the status quo is maintained.
- Isolate the potential problem linked to lack of performance, such as noncompliance issues, poor safety record, or the inability to take on additional projects.
- Identify the specific measure that reflects the potential problem.
- Pinpoint the anticipated "problem" level of the measure if no program is implemented (for example, industry average, benchmarking data).
- Calculate the difference in the measure from current levels desired and the potential "problem" level of the measure. This becomes the change that could occur if the program is not implemented.
- Develop the unit value of the measure using standard values, expert input, or external databases.
- Develop an estimate of the total potential value. This becomes the total expected value of benefits derived from implementing the program.
- Estimate the total cost of the proposed HR program using the techniques outlined in earlier in this chapter.
- Compare projected benefits with costs.

An example shows how this process can be used. An organization has an excellent record of avoiding discrimination lawsuits, and HR executives want to maintain it. The industry average shows that discrimination charges occur at a rate of two complaints per 1,000 employees per year. This company has a record average of only 0.25 complaints per 1,000 employees—far below the industry average. The organization would like to implement a diversity program to continue to focus attention on this critical issue and ensure that the current, acceptable rate does not deteriorate.

The first challenge is to define the specific measure based on charges filed with the EEOC. The cost of a discrimination charge averages $35,000, according to government and legal databases. Using this as a measure, the payoff for the program is the funds lost if the organization's current average migrated to the industry average. For the company's 4,000-employee workforce, the movement would be from one complaint (the company's average) to eight complaints (the industry average). Thus, the value of seven complaints is 7 x $35,000, or $245,000. This figure represents the potential savings of maintaining the current level of charges, assuming that the company's rate of complaints would rise to the industry level if no program were implemented.

The cost of the program can easily be compared with this monetary value to arrive at the potential payoff. In reality, the rate of charges may never reach the industry average because of present company practices. If this is the situation, a discounted value could be developed. For example, 75% of the industry average could be used as the potential value achieved if no program were implemented.

This approach has some disadvantages. The potential loss of value (income or cost savings) can be highly subjective and difficult to measure. Because of these concerns, this approach to evaluating the return on HR investments is limited to certain types of situations. This approach has some advantages, particularly with the focus on a variety of preventive programs. It provides a vehicle to use the ROI methodology in situations where the status quo is acceptable and represents best practices. The approach can show the value of investing in new programs to maintain a current favorable position. Essentially, the steps are the same. The challenge is to determine where the measure would be positioned if no program were implemented.

Cautions When Using ROI

Because of the sensitivity of the ROI methodology, caution is needed when developing, calculating, and communicating ROI. The implementation of ROI is an important issue and a goal of many HR departments. A few issues should be addressed to keep the process from going astray:

■ *Remember to take a conservative approach when developing both benefits and costs.* Conservatism in ROI analysis builds accuracy and credibility. What matters most is how the target audience perceives the value of the data. A conservative approach is always recommended for both the numerator of the ROI formula (net benefits) and the denominator (program costs). The conservative approach is the basis for the guiding principles.

- *Be careful when comparing the ROI in HR with other financial returns.* There are several ways to calculate the return on funds invested or assets employed. ROI is just one of them. Although the calculation for ROI in HR uses the same basic formula as in other investment evaluations, it may not be fully understood by the audience. Its calculation method and its meaning should be clearly communicated. More important, it should be an item accepted by management as an appropriate measure for HR program evaluation.

- *Involve management in developing the return.* Management ultimately makes the decision if an ROI value is acceptable. To the extent possible, management should be involved in setting the parameters for calculations and establishing targets by which programs are considered acceptable within the organization.

- *Fully disclose assumptions and methodology.* When discussing the ROI methodology and communicating data, it is important that you be straightforward about the process, steps, and assumptions used in the process. Communicate clearly the strengths, weaknesses, confidence levels, and shortcomings of the ROI evaluation.

- *Approach sensitive and controversial issues with caution.* Occasionally, sensitive and controversial issues will be generated when discussing an ROI value. It is best to avoid debates over what is measurable and what is not measurable during a presentation of a study. Debates should occur early in the process. Some programs may involve politically sensitive issues that must be considered early and often in the analysis and reporting. Also, some programs are so fundamental to the survival of the organization that any attempt to measure them is unnecessary. For example, a program designed to improve customer service in a customer-focused company may escape the scrutiny of an ROI evaluation on the assumption that if the program is well designed, it will improve customer service.

- *Teach others the methods for calculating ROI.* Each time an ROI is calculated, the HR manager should use the opportunity to educate other managers, colleagues, and the HR staff. Although measurement may not be in their area of responsibility, these individuals will be able to see the value of this approach to HR evaluation. Also, when possible, each project should serve as a case study to educate the HR staff on specific techniques and methods.

- *Recognize, however, that not everyone will buy into ROI.* Not every audience member will understand, appreciate, or accept the ROI calculation. For a variety of reasons, one or more individuals may not agree with the input values. These individuals may be highly emotional about the concept of showing accountability for HR. Attempts to persuade them may be beyond the scope of the task at hand.

■ *Don't boast about a high return.* It is not unusual to generate what appears to be a very high ROI for an HR program. Several examples in this book have illustrated the possibilities. An HR manager who boasts about a high rate of return is open to potential criticism from others unless there are indisputable facts on which the calculation is based. In addition, future programs may not generate the same high ROIs, possibly leaving the manager with a sense of failure and the target audience with feelings of unmet expectations.

■ *Choose the time and place for the debates.* The time to debate the ROI methodology is not during a presentation unless it cannot be avoided. There are constructive times to debate the ROI process: in a special forum, among the HR staff, in an educational session, in professional literature, on panel discussions, or even during the development of an ROI impact study. Select the setting and timing for debates with care so as not to detract from the quality and quantity of information presented.

■ *Do not attempt to use ROI on all HR programs.* As discussed earlier, the value of some programs is difficult to quantify, and an ROI calculation may not be feasible. Other methods of presenting the benefits may be more appropriate.

Final Thoughts

Costs are important for a variety of uses and applications. They help the HR staff manage the resources carefully, consistently, and efficiently. They also allow for comparisons between different elements and cost categories. Cost categorization can take several different forms; the most common are presented in this chapter. Costs should be fully loaded for ROI calculation. From a practical standpoint, including certain cost items may be optional, based on the organization's guidelines and philosophy. Nevertheless, because of the scrutiny involved in ROI calculations, it is recommended that all costs be included, even if they go beyond the requirements of the company policy.

After you collect data on program benefits, convert them to monetary values, and develop a fully loaded cost profile, the ROI calculation becomes an easy next step. It is just a matter of plugging the values into the formula. This chapter has presented the two basic approaches for calculating the return—BCR and the ROI formulas. You also had an opportunity to read about some case studies that utilized the ROI methodology. Finally, the chapter highlighted some issues and cautions that you must keep in mind when performing ROI calculations.

CHAPTER 7

Measuring Intangibles

Intangible measures are the nonmonetary benefits or detriments directly linked to HR that cannot or should not be converted to monetary values. These measures are often monitored after an HR program has been implemented, and, although not converted to monetary values, they are still important in the evaluation process. Although the range of intangible measures is almost limitless, this chapter describes a few common measures that are often linked with HR (Table 24).

Table 24. Typical Intangible Variables Linked with HR Programs[14]

- Employee Satisfaction
- Organizational Commitment
- Culture
- Climate
- Diversity
- Employee Complaints
- Grievances
- Discrimination Complaints
- Stress
- Wellness/Fitness
- Employee Retention
- Employee Absenteeism
- Employee Tardiness
- Employee Transfers

- Leadership
- Ethics
- Image
- Customer Satisfaction Survey Data
- Customer Complaints
- Customer Loyalty
- Teamwork
- Cooperation
- Conflict
- Decisiveness
- Communication
- Innovation and Creativity
- Competencies

Key Concepts about Intangibles

By design, some measures are captured and reported as intangible measures. Although they may not be perceived to be as valuable as the measures converted to monetary values, intangible measures are critical to the overall success of the organization.

In such programs as diversity enhancement, retention improvement, innovation and creativity, leadership development, and customer service, intangible (nonmonetary) benefits can be more important than tangible (monetary) measures. Consequently, intangible measures should be monitored and reported as part of the overall evaluation. In practice, every project or program, regardless of its nature, scope, and content, has intangible measures associated with it; the challenge is to identify and report them efficiently.

Tangibles and Intangibles: What's the Difference?

Perhaps the first step to understanding intangibles is to clearly define the difference between tangible and intangible assets in a business organization. As shown in Table 25, tangible assets are required for business oper-

Table 25. Comparison of Tangible and Intangible Assets[15]

Tangible Assets— Required for Business Operations	Intangible Assets— Key to Competitive Advantage in the Knowledge Area
■ Readily visible ■ Rigorously quantified ■ Part of the balance sheet ■ Investment produces known returns ■ Can be easily duplicated ■ Depreciates with use ■ Has finite application ■ Best managed with "scarcity" mentality ■ Best leveraged through control ■ Can be accumulated	■ Invisible ■ Difficult to quantify ■ Not tracked through accounting practices ■ Assessment based on assumptions ■ Cannot be bought or imitated ■ Appreciates with purposeful use ■ Multi-application without reducing value ■ Best managed with "abundance" mentality ■ Best leveraged through alignment ■ Dynamic: short shelf life when not in use

ations, readily visible, rigorously quantified, and routinely represented as line items on balance sheets (Saint-Onge, 2002). The intangible assets are the key to competitive advantage. They are invisible, difficult to quantify, and not tracked through traditional accounting practices. With this distinction, it is easy to understand why intangible measures are difficult to convert to monetary values.

Another basis for the distinction between tangible and intangible assets is the concept of hard data versus soft data. This concept, discussed earlier, is perhaps more familiar to HR practitioners. Table 26 shows the difference between hard and soft data. The most significant part of the definition of soft data lies in the *difficulty in converting* the data to monetary value. Intangible measures are defined as measures that are *purposely not converted* to monetary values. Using this simple definition avoids confusion of whether a data item should be classified as hard data or soft data. It is considered soft data if a credible, economically feasible process is unavailable for conversion. The ROI methodology discussed throughout this book uses this definition of intangibles.

Table 26. Characteristics of Data[16]

Hard Data	Soft Data
■ Objectively based	■ Subjectively based in many cases
■ Easy to measure and quantify	■ Difficult to measure and quantify, directly
■ Relatively easy to assign monetary values	■ Difficult to assign monetary values
■ Common measures of organizational performance	■ Less credible as a performance measure
■ Very credible with management	■ Usually behaviorally oriented

Identification of Measures

Data on intangible measures are available from different sources representing different timeframes, as illustrated in Figure 17. First, **you can uncover them early in the process, during the needs assessment and initial**

analysis. Once you have identified the sources, you can plan to collect intangible data as part of the overall data collection strategy. For example, a new reward systems program may have several hard data measures, such as productivity and quality, linked to the program. Employee satisfaction is an intangible measure that you can identify and monitor without any intention or plan for converting it to a monetary value. Therefore, from the very beginning, this measure is destined to be a nonmonetary benefit reported along with the ROI results.

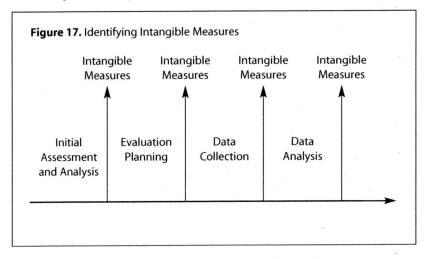

Figure 17. Identifying Intangible Measures

Second, **you can identify intangible measures during discussions with clients or sponsors about the impact of an HR program.** Clients can usually identify intangible measures that are expected to be influenced by the program. For example, a large multinational company implemented a wellness and fitness program and then planned for an ROI analysis. During the ROI planning session, program designers, the contractor, and a senior executive identified potential intangible measures that were perceived to be influenced by the program. These measures were included on the ROI analysis planning document.

Third, **you can identify intangible measures during a follow-up evaluation.** Perhaps a measure is not expected or anticipated in the initial program design, but it surfaces later on a questionnaire, in an interview, or during a focus group. These data collection methods often include questions about other improvements linked to the HR program. Participant responses often provide several intangible measures and there are no planned attempts to place a value on the actual measure.

For example, in an innovation and creativity program, participants were asked specifically what had improved in their work as a result of the program. The participants provided several intangible measures, which managers perceived to be linked to the program.

Fourth, **you can identify intangible measures during an attempt to convert the data to monetary values.** If the conversion process loses credibility, the measure should be reported as an intangible benefit. For example, in a customer relationship management program, customer satisfaction is identified early in the process as one of the measures of program success. A conversion of the data to monetary values was attempted. However, the process of assigning a value to the data diminished the credibility of the analysis; therefore, customer satisfaction was reported as an intangible benefit.

Is It Measurable?

Sometimes a debate erupts over whether a particular item perceived as intangible (soft) can actually be measured. In reality, any item that represents the outcome of an HR program can be measured. The measure may have to be a perception of the issue taken from a stakeholder involved in the process, but it is still a measure. The ROI methodology rests on the assumption that anything can be measured. In the mind of the sponsor or senior executive, if an intangible (soft) item cannot be measured, why bother? The state of the situation or issue will never be known if it cannot be measured. Thus, on a practical basis, any intangible can be measured—some precisely, others not very precisely. For example, the number of team conflicts is a measure that can be assessed and categorized. HR staff can record all conflicts observed and place them into categories. However, to place a value on a conflict may cause the data item to be labeled intangible if no credible, economically feasible way is available to convert it to monetary value.

Can It Be Converted?

Chapter 5 focused on various ways to convert data to monetary values. The philosophy is simple: Any data item can be converted to monetary value; there is no measure to which a monetary value cannot be assigned. The key issue is credibility of the converted value. Is it a believable value? Is a credible process used to convert data to monetary values? Does it cost too much to convert the data to monetary value? Is that value stable over time? Senior executives weigh these critical issues as they examine the conversion of data to monetary value. For tangible data conversion, the issue is of little concern. Tangible data items, such as increased output, reduction in rejects, and time savings, are easily converted. Soft measures (stress, complaints, attitudes, and so forth), however, tend to lose credibility in the conversion process.

Table 27 shows a four-part test for converting intangibles to monetary values. This is the test that often leads to the classification of data as intangible. The ultimate question is posted in step 4, which is a practical issue that protects the credibility of the impact study and also allows for consistency from one study to another. The ROI methodology would be unreliable if one evaluator converted a particular data item to monetary value whereas another evaluator did not. Maintaining this consistency is an important part of building the standards necessary for the ROI methodology.

Table 27. Test for Converting Intangibles to Monetary Value

1. Does an acceptable, standard monetary value exist for the measure? If yes, use it; if not, go to step 2.
2. Is there a method you can use to convert the measure to money? If not, list it as an intangible; if yes, go to step 3.
3. Can you accomplish the conversion with minimum resources? If not, list it as an intangible; if yes, go to step 4.
4. Can you describe the conversion process to an executive audience and secure buy-in in two minutes? If yes, use it in the ROI calculation; if not, list it as an intangible.

Intangible Measures versus Intellectual Capital

In recent years, considerable attention has been given to the concept of intellectual capital and the value of intangible assets in organizations. Intellectual capital typically involves customer capital, human capital, and structural capital (Phillips, 2002). It is helpful to distinguish between the intangible measures from an HR program and those that might appear in a variety of measures in intellectual capital. Figure 18 shows the categories of intangible assets and their relationship to intellectual capital.

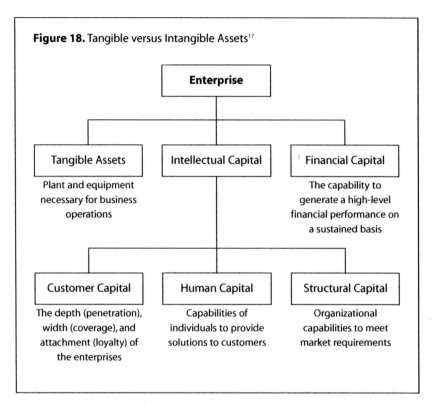

Figure 18. Tangible versus Intangible Assets[17]

Analysis

For most intangible data, no specific analysis is planned. Any previous attempts to convert intangible data to monetary units would have been unsuccessful. In some cases, you may attempt to isolate the effects of the HR program using one or more of the methods outlined in Chapter 5. This step is necessary when there is a need to know the specific amount of change in the intangible measure that is linked to the program. In many cases, however, the intangible data reflect evidence of improvement. You do not need either the precise amount of the improvement or the amount of improvement related directly to the HR program. Because the value of the intangible data is not plugged into the ROI calculation, intangible measures normally are not used to justify addition of programs or continuation of existing programs. Consequently, a detailed analysis is not necessary. Intangible benefits provide supporting evidence of the program success and can be presented as qualitative data.

Typical Intangible Measures

Most of the remainder of the chapter focuses on typical intangible measures. These measures are often presented as intangibles in impact studies. In some cases, organizations do convert intangible data to monetary values. Here are three examples, which are covered in more detail in this section, along with several others:

■   Retention (employee turnover) is now converted to monetary value in most cases and presented as a tangible.
■   Reliable ways are available to arrive at the value for absenteeism without exhausting resources.
■   Also, recent developments in the measurement of customer satisfaction provide ways to convert this critical measure to monetary value.

Employee Satisfaction

Employee satisfaction is perhaps one of the most important intangible measures. Improving job satisfaction is the goal of a variety of HR programs. Organizations carry out attitude surveys to measure the extent to which employees are satisfied with the organization, their jobs, their supervisor, co-workers, and a host of other job-related factors. For example, in a vision and values program implemented for all employees at one organization, the annual attitude survey contained five questions directly tied to perceptions and attitudes influenced by the program.

Because attitude surveys are usually taken annually, survey results may not be in sync with the timing of a specific HR program. When employee satisfaction is one of the program objectives and is a critical outcome, some organizations conduct surveys at a prescribed timeframe after the HR program is implemented and design the survey instrument around issues related to the program. This approach, however, is expensive.

Although employee satisfaction has always been an important issue in employee relations, in recent years it has taken on increased importance because of the correlation between job satisfaction and other key measures. A classic relationship with employee satisfaction is in the area of employee recruitment and retention. Firms with excellent employee satisfaction ratings are often attractive to potential employees. The high ratings become a subtle but important recruiting tool. "Employers of Choice" and "Best Places to Work," for example, often have high levels of employee satisfaction ratings, which attract employees.

The significance of the relationship between employee satisfaction and employee turnover has grown as turnover and retention have become critical issues in the last decade and are likely to remain so in the future. The relationship is easily developed with current HR information systems, which have modules to calculate the correlation between the turnover rates and the employee satisfaction scores for the various job groups, divisions, departments, and so forth.

Employee satisfaction has an important connection to customer service. Hundreds of applied research projects are beginning to show a very high correlation between employee satisfaction scores and customer satisfaction scores. These links, often referred to as service-profit chain, create a promising way to identify important relationships between attitudes and profits in an organization.

Even with these developments, most organizations do not or cannot place credible values on employee satisfaction data. The trend is moving in the right direction, but, for now, job satisfaction is usually listed as an intangible benefit in impact studies.

Organizational Commitment/Engagement

In recent years, organizational commitment (OC) measures have complemented or replaced job satisfaction measures. OC measures go beyond employee satisfaction and include the extent to which the employees identify with organizational goals, mission, philosophy, value, policies, and practices. The concept of involvement and engagement with the organization is the key issue. OC is a measure that closely correlates with productivity and other performance improvement measures, in contrast to employee satisfaction, which does not always correlate with improvements in productivity. As OC scores improve (according to a standard index), a corresponding improvement in productivity should develop. The OC is often measured the same way as attitude surveys, using a five- or seven-point scale taken directly from employees or groups of employees.

OC is rarely converted to monetary value. Although some relationships have been developed to link it to more tangible data, this research is still in development. For most studies, OC would be listed as an intangible.

Culture

In recent years, much attention has been focused on the culture of the organization. Culture is a function of the organization's practices, beliefs, opinions, behaviors, policies, vision, and values. Various HR-driven culture change projects attempt to strengthen, solidify, or adjust the culture. The culture in some organizations is distinct and defined, but it is always difficult to measure precisely.

Some organizations use culture instruments to collect data on this measure before and after an HR program to measure improvement. The scores on these instruments represent important data that may connect directly to the HR program. In practice, it is difficult to convert culture data to monetary value in a credible way. Therefore, culture change is usually listed as an intangible measure.

Climate

Some organizations conduct climate surveys, which reflect work climate changes such as communication, openness, trust, and quality of feedback. Closely related to organizational commitment and culture, climate surveys are more general and often focus on a range of workplace issues and environmental enablers and inhibitors. Climate surveys conducted before and after an HR program is implemented may reflect the extent to which the program has changed these intangible measures.

Diversity

Diversity continues to important as organizations strive to develop and nurture a diverse workforce. HR-initiated programs influence the diversity mix of the organization, and a variety of data is available to measure the impact of focusing on diversity. The diversity mix is a measure showing employee categories along diversity definitions such as race, creed, color, national origin, age, religion, and sex. This diversity mix shows the makeup of the team at any given time and is not a measure that can be converted to monetary value credibly.

The payoff of having a diverse group influences several other measures including absenteeism, turnover, discrimination complaints, morale, and sometimes productivity and quality. Also, a variety of diversity perception instruments are available to measure the attitudes of employees toward diversity issues; they are often administered before and after diversity projects. In addition, some organizations collect input on diversity issues in an annual feedback survey. All of these measures are important and reveal progress on an important issue, but they are difficult to convert directly to monetary value and are usually listed as intangibles.

Employee Complaints

Some organizations record and report specific employee complaints. These feedback mechanisms are usually highly visible and have catchy names such as "Speak Out," "Talk Back," or "Hey, Mike" (in an organization where the CEO's first name is Mike). A reduction in the number of employee complaints is sometimes directly related to an HR program, such as a team-building program. Consequently, the level of complaints is used as a measure of the program's success and is usually reported as an intangible measure. Because of the difficulty in converting complaints to monetary values, this measure is almost always listed as an intangible benefit.

Grievances

In both union and non-union organizations, grievances reflect the level of dissatisfaction or disenchantment with a variety of factors in the organization. Sometimes, HR programs, such as labor-management cooperation, are designed to reduce the number of grievances when the figure is considered too high. An improvement in the grievance level may reflect the success of the program. The impact of grievances can be significant and affect a variety of cost categories. Although this measure may be converted to a monetary value, as described in Chapter 5, it is usually reported as an intangible measure.

Discrimination Complaints

Employee dissatisfaction appears in different types of discrimination complaints, ranging from informal complaints to external charges and even litigation against the organization. HR programs, such as a sexual harassment prevention program, can be designed to prevent complaints or to reduce the current level of complaint activity. This measure can be devastating to organizations. However, the success of the program, in terms of complaint reduction, is sometimes not converted to monetary values because of the various assumptions and estimates involved in the process. When this is the case, these measures are reported as intangible program benefits.

Stress Reduction

HR programs such as work/life balance, personal productivity, or conflict resolution can reduce work-related stress by preparing employees to identify and confront stress factors to improve job performance, accomplish more in a workday, and relieve tension and anxiety. The subsequent reduction in stress may be directly linked to the program. Although excessive stress may be directly linked to other, easy-to-convert data, such as productivity, absenteeism, and medical claims, it is usually listed as an intangible benefit.

Employee Retention

When employee satisfaction deteriorates to the point that employees withdraw from work or the organization, either permanently or temporarily, the results can be disastrous. Perhaps the most critical employee withdrawal variable is employee turnover (or employee attrition).

An extremely costly variable, turnover can have devastating consequences on organizations when it is excessive. Few measures have attracted so much attention as employee turnover. Fueled in part by low unemployment rates in North America and other industrialized countries, retention has become a strategic issue. The survival of some firms depends on low turnover rates for critical job groups (Phillips and Connell, 2003). Not only is turnover compared to historical rates, but it is often compared to best practice firms.

The good news is that many firms have made important strides in maintaining low turnover rates even in high-turnover industries such as retail, hotel, and restaurant industries. Turnover is defined as the number of employees leaving in a month divided by the average number of employees in the month. This is a standard turnover rate that includes all individuals leaving the organization. A more appropriate measure would be to include only turnover considered to be avoidable, usually referring to employees who voluntarily leave or those whose departure could have been prevented. For example, if an employee is terminated for poor performance in the first six months of employment, something went wrong that could have been prevented. Avoidable turnover is an important issue.

Many HR programs are designed to improve retention. In most situations, turnover is actually converted to monetary values, using one of the methods described in Chapter 5. However, because of the multitude of costs and assumptions involved in developing the value, some organizations prefer not to convert turnover to a monetary value. In this case, turnover is reported as an intangible benefit, reflecting the success of the HR program.

Employee Absenteeism

Unplanned absenteeism is another disruptive and costly variable. Many HR programs are designed to reduce absenteeism; it is usually possible to pinpoint the amount of absenteeism reduction related to the program. Although the cost of absenteeism can be developed, the variety of costs—direct and indirect—necessary for a fully loaded cost impact makes the process difficult. Consequently, the conversion process is not credible enough for some audiences, and absenteeism changes are reported as intangible benefits.

Employee Tardiness

Some organizations actually monitor tardiness, especially in highly focused work and tightly contained work environments, such as call centers. Tardiness is an irritating work habit that can cause inefficiencies and delays. Organizations can use electronic and computerized time reporting to identify problem areas. A few HR programs are designed to reduce or prevent it. Tardiness is very difficult to convert to a monetary value because of the many aspects of the impact of the unacceptable work habit. Consequently, when tardiness is presented as an improvement from an HR program, it is usually listed as an intangible benefit.

Employee Transfers

Another way for employees to withdraw is to request a transfer to another section, department, or division of the organization. Requests for transfers often reflect dissatisfaction with a variety of issues including management, policies, and practices in the organization. Transfers are essentially internal turnover. Some HR programs aim to reduce or remove these unpleasant environmental influences. In such situations, requests for transfers are monitored and reported as an intangible benefit of the HR program. Although it is possible to place a value on this internal turnover, usually no attempt is made to assign monetary values to transfers.

Innovation and Creativity

For many progressive organizations, innovation is important to success. A variety of innovation and creativity programs are implemented to improve this critical area. Innovation is a paradox in that it is both easy and difficult to measure. It is easy to measure outcomes in areas such as copyrights, patents, inventions, new projects, and employee suggestions. It is more difficult to measure the creative spirit and behavior of employees.

An employee suggestion system, a longtime measure of the innovative and creative processes of an organization, still flourishes today in many firms. Employees are rewarded for their suggestions if they are approved and implemented. Tracking the suggestion rates and comparing them with other organizations is an important benchmarking item for innovation and creative capability. Other measures, such as the number of new projects, products, processes, and strategies, can be monitored and measured in some way.

Some organizations actually measure the creative spirit of employees using inventories and instruments. Comparing scores of groups of employees over time reflects the degree to which employees are improving innovativeness and creativity in the workplace. Subjectivity often enters the measurement process with these issues. Having consistent and comparable measures is still a challenge. Because of the difficulty of converting data to monetary values, these measures are usually listed as intangibles.

Competencies

Organizations are interested in developing key competencies in particular areas such as the core mission, key product lines, and important processes. Core competencies are often identified and implemented in critical job groups. It is possible to measure competencies with self-assessments from the individual employee as well as with assessments from their supervisors. In some cases, other inputs may be important or necessary to measure. That approach goes beyond just learning new skills, processes, or knowledge to using a combination of skills, knowledge, and behavior on the job to develop an acceptable level of competence to meet competitive challenges. Because of the difficulty in converting competencies to monetary values, measures of improvement are often left as intangible.

Leadership

Perhaps the most difficult measure is leadership. Effective leadership can make the difference between the success and failure of an organization. Without appropriate leadership behaviors throughout the organization, resources can be misapplied or wasted.

It is possible to measure leadership with any of several instruments and inventories for assessing the leadership style, preference, or practice of managers. These inventories yield profiles that can be monitored over time and compared to expectations or desired level. The instruments also can assess the current leadership style and can be related to expectations and targets.

One of the most common methods is known as 360-degree feedback. Here, a prescribed set of leadership behaviors desired in an organization is assessed by different sources to provide a composite of the overall leadership capability. The sources often include the immediate manager of the leader, a colleague in the same area, the employees under the direct influence of the leader, internal or external customers, and self-assessment. These assessments come from different directions, forming a 360-degree circle. The measure is basically an observation captured in a survey, often reported electronically. 360-degree feedback has been growing rapidly in the United States, Europe, and Asia as an important way to capture overall leadership behavior change, but it is usually left as an intangible.

Ethics

In the wake of a variety of business scandals in recent years, the issue of ethics has gained a higher level of interest and priority in organizations. Several HR-driven programs focus on shaping the desired ethical behavior and conduct. The menu of available programs ranges from briefings to policies to role modeling to training. Also, these programs often provide an opportunity for employees to use hotlines or special contacts to expose unethical practices. While measures are available to show improvements in ethical behavior (or the perception of improvement) these measures are often not converted to monetary value but left as intangibles.

Customer Satisfaction

Because of the importance of building and improving customer service, several measures are often monitored and reported as a payoff of an HR program. HR-driven customer service programs have a direct influence on these measures. One of the most important measures is survey data showing the degree to which customers are pleased with the products and services. These survey values, reported as absolute data or as an index, represent important data from which to compare the success of a customer service program.

As described earlier, customer satisfaction data are attracting much interest. The data's value is often linked to other measures such as revenue growth, market share, and profits. Several models are available to show what happens when customers are dissatisfied, along with the economic impact of those decisions. Even in the health care area, researchers are showing linkages between patient satisfaction and customer retention. Still others are demonstrating relationships between customer satisfaction and such measures as innovation, product development, and some tangibles. Techniques are available to convert survey data to monetary values, but, in most situations, the conversion is rarely attempted. Consequently, customer satisfaction improvements at the present time are usually reported as intangible benefits.

Customer Complaints

Most organizations monitor customer complaints. Each complaint is recorded along with the disposition and the time required to resolve the complaint, as well as specific costs associated with the complaint resolution. Organizations sometimes design HR programs to reduce the number of customer complaints. The total cost and impact of a complaint has three components:

- the time it takes to resolve the complaint;
- the cost of making restitution to the customer; and
- the ultimate cost of ill will generated by the dissatisfaction (lost future business).

Because of the difficulty of assigning an accurate monetary value to a customer complaint, the measure usually becomes a very important intangible benefit.

Customer Loyalty

Customer retention is a critical measure that is sometimes linked to sales, marketing, and customer service programs. Long-term, efficient, and productive customer relationships are important to the success of an organization. Although the importance of customer retention is understood, it is not always converted to monetary value. Specific models can show the value of a customer and the value of keeping customers over a period of time. For example, the average tenure of a customer can translate directly into bottom-line profits.

Tied closely to customer loyalty is the rate at which customers leave the organization. This churn rate is a critical measure that can be costly not only in lost business (profits from lost customers), but also the cost necessary to generate a new customer. Because of the difficulty of converting directly to a specific monetary value, customer loyalty usually is listed as an intangible benefit.

Other Customer Responses

It is possible to track a variety of other types of customer responses, too, including creativity with customer response, customer response time, responsiveness to cost and pricing issues, and other important issues customers may specify or require. Monitoring these variables can provide more evidence of an HR program's results when the program influences specific variables. Because of the difficulty of assigning values to the items, they are usually reported as intangible measures.

Teamwork

You can monitor various measures that reflect how well teams are working. Although the output of teams and the quality of their work are often measured as hard data and converted to monetary values, you can monitor and report other interpersonal measures, too. Sometimes organizations survey team members before and after an HR program to determine if the level of teamwork has increased. Using a variable scale, team members provide a perception of improvement. The monetary value of increased teamwork is rarely developed, and, consequently, it is reported as an intangible benefit.

Cooperation

The success of a team often depends on the cooperative spirit of team members. Some instruments measure the level of cooperation before and after the implementation of an HR program using a perception scale. Because of the difficulty of converting this measure to a monetary value, it is almost always reported as an intangible benefit.

Conflict

In team environments, the level of conflict is sometimes measured. A reduction in conflict may reflect the success of an HR initiative. Although conflict reduction can be measured by perception or numbers of conflicts, the monetary value is an illusive figure. Consequently, in most situations, a monetary value is not placed on conflict reduction, and it is reported as an intangible benefit.

Decisiveness

Teams make decisions, and the timing of the decision-making process often becomes an issue. Consequently, decisiveness is sometimes measured in terms of the speed at which decisions are made. Some HR programs are expected to influence this process. Survey measures may reflect the perception of the team or, in some cases, monitor how quickly decisions are made. Although reductions in the timing of decisions can be converted to monetary values, improvements are usually reported as intangible benefits.

Communication

Communication instruments and inventories reflect the quality and quantity of communication within a team. Improvements in communications or perceptions of effectiveness driven by an HR program are not usually converted to monetary values and are reported as intangible benefits.

Final Thoughts

Dozens of intangible measures are available to reflect the success of HR programs. Although they may not be perceived to be as useful as specific monetary measures, they are, nevertheless, an important part of an overall evaluation. Intangible measures should be identified, explored, examined, monitored, and analyzed for changes when they are linked to the program. Collectively, intangibles add a unique dimension to the overall program results because most, if not all, programs have intangible measures associated with them. Some of the most common intangible measures were covered in this chapter, but the coverage was not meant to be complete.

CHAPTER 8

Communicating and Using Evaluation Data

Okay, you have your data in hand, so what's next? Should the data be used to modify the program, change the process, show the contribution, justify new programs, gain additional support, or build goodwill? How should the data be presented? Who should present the data? Where and when should the data be communicated? This chapter delves into these and other questions, but most important, this chapter tells you how evaluation data, properly communicated to the right audiences, can drive improvement in your organization.

Principles of Communicating Results

The skills required to communicate results effectively are almost as delicate and sophisticated as those needed to obtain results. Style is as important as the substance. Regardless of the message, audience, or medium, a few general principles apply. Because they are important to the overall success of the communication effort, these principles should serve as a checklist for the HR staff when disseminating program results.

Communication Must Be Timely

In general, you should communicate results as soon as they are known. From a practical standpoint, it may be best to delay the communication until a convenient time, such as the next management meeting, quarterly sales meeting, or annual HR conference. Address issues of timing: Is the audience ready for the results considering other things that may have happened? Is the audience expecting results? When is the best time for having the maximum effect on the audience? Are there circumstances that dictate a change in the timing of the communication?

Communication Should Be Targeted to Specific Audiences

Communication is more effective if it is designed for a particular group. The message should be specifically tailored to the interests, needs, and expectations of the target audience. The results described in this chapter reflect outcomes at all levels of evaluation. When results are communicated depends in part on what the data are developed. The data developed early in the project can be communicated during the project. Data collected after implementation can be communicated in a follow-up study. Therefore, the results, in their broadest sense, range from early feedback with qualitative data to ROI values in various quantitative terms.

Media Should Be Carefully Selected

For particular groups, some media are more effective than others. Face-to-face meetings may be better than special bulletins. A memo distributed exclusively to top management may be more effective than the company's newsletter. Choosing the most appropriate method of communication can help improve the effectiveness of the process.

Communication Should Be Unbiased and Modest

Facts must be separated from fiction and accurate statements must be separated from opinions. Some audiences are likely to be skeptical about accepting communication from the HR staff because they anticipate receiving biased opinions. Boastful statements sometimes turn off recipients, and most—if not all—of the content's significance is lost. Observable, credible facts carry far more weight than extreme or sensational claims. Although such claims may get audience attention, they often detract from the importance of the results.

Communication Must Be Consistent

The timing and content of the communication should be consistent with past practices. A special communication at an unusual time during the program may provoke suspicion. Also, if a particular group, such as top management, regularly receives communication on outcomes, it should continue receiving communication—even if the results are not positive. If some results are omitted, it might leave the impression that only positive results are reported.

Confidentiality and Privacy Are Paramount

The reputation of the HR staff is an important consideration. Negative comments or sensitive feedback may be detrimental to the source if not protected properly. Data should be treated confidentially to protect the privacy of individuals. Data should be combined in such a way that an individual's responses cannot be identified. HR staff must strive to maintain a high level of credibility and respect when communicating results. Never jeopardize your credibility by compromising people's privacy.

Planning the Communication Is Critical

Carefully plan communication to produce the maximum results. Planning ensures that each audience receives the proper information at the right time and that appropriate actions are taken. Table 28 shows the areas that will need attention as you develop the communication plan.

Table 28. Communication Planning Questions

Who are the target audiences?

What will actually be communicated?

When will the data be communicated?

How will the information be communicated?

Where will the communication take place?

Who will communicate the information?

What specific actions are required or desired?

These general principles are important to the overall success of the communication effort. They should serve as a checklist for the HR staff when disseminating program results.

Selecting the Audience for Communications

To the greatest extent possible, the HR staff should know and understand the target audience. The staff should find out what information is needed and why. Each group has its own needs relative to the information desired. Some seek detailed information, and others want brief information. You may need input from others to determine audience needs. The staff should try to understand audience bias. The staff should be empathetic and try to understand differing views. With this understanding, communications can be tailored to each group. This is especially critical when the potential exists for the audience to react negatively to the results. The questions presented in Table 29 should be addressed when selecting the audience.

Table 29. Key Questions for Selecting Audiences

Are they interested in the program?
Do they really want to receive the information?
Has someone already made a commitment to them regarding communication?
Is the timing right for this audience?
Are they familiar with the program?
How do they prefer to have results communicated?
Do they know the team members?
Are they likely to find the results threatening?
Which medium will be most convincing to this group?

The potential target audiences who are to receive information about results have different job levels and responsibilities. One way to select your audiences is to analyze the reason behind the communication. Table 30 shows common target audiences and the basis for selecting the audience.

Perhaps the most important audience is the sponsor—the individual or team supporting the evaluation. This audience initiates the program, reviews data, and weighs the final assessment of the effectiveness of the program. Another important target audience is the top management group. This group is responsible for allocating resources for the HR program and needs information to help justify expenditures and gauge the effectiveness of the efforts.

Selected groups of managers (or all managers) are also important target audiences. Management's support and involvement in the process and the department's credibility are important to success. Effectively communicating program results to management can increase both support and credibility.

Table 30. Rationale for Specific Target Audiences

Reason for Communication	Primary Target Audiences
To secure approval for the program	Sponsor, Top Executives
To gain support for the program	Managers, Team Leaders
To secure agreement with the issues	Participants, Team Leaders
To build credibility for Human Resources	Top Executives, Managers
To enhance reinforcement of the processes	Immediate Managers
To drive action for improvement	Sponsor, Human Resources Staff
To prepare participants for the program	Team Leaders, Participants
To enhance results and quality of future feedback	Participants
To show the complete results of the HR program	Sponsor, Human Resources Staff
To underscore the importance of measuring results	Sponsor, Human Resources Staff
To explain techniques used to results	Sponsor, Human Resources Staff
To create desire for a participant to be involved	Team Leaders, Participants
To stimulate interest in Human Resources	Top Executives, Managers
To demonstrate accountability for expenditures	All Employees
To market future programs	Prospective Sponsors, Managers, Team Leaders

Communicating with the participants' team leaders (or immediate managers) is essential. In many cases, team leaders must encourage participants to implement the program. Also, they often support and reinforce the objectives of the program. Positive results enhance the commitment to HR and improve credibility for the HR staff.

Occasionally, you may communicate results to encourage participation in the program. This approach is especially effective for programs that employees attend on a voluntary basis. The potential participants are important targets for communicating results.

Participants (stakeholders) need feedback on the overall success of the effort. Some individuals may not have been as successful as others in achieving the desired results. Communicating the results adds additional pressure to effectively implement the program and improve results for the future. For those achieving excellent results, communication serves as a reinforcement of what is expected. Communicating results to participants is often overlooked because it is assumed that because the program is complete, participants do not need to be informed of its success.

The HR staff needs communication about program results. Those who designed, developed, and implemented the program must know about the program's effectiveness so that adjustments can be made if necessary. The support staff should receive detailed information about the process to measure results. This group provides support services to the HR team.

All employees and stockholders are less likely targets. General interest news stories may increase employee respect for HR. Goodwill and positive attitudes toward the organization may also be by-products of communicating results. Stockholders, on the other hand, are more interested in the return on their investment.

Table 30 shows the most common target audiences, although there can be others in a particular organization. For example, management or employees could be divided into different departments, divisions, or even subsidiaries of the organization. The number of audiences can be large in a complex organization. At a minimum, you should communicate to four target audiences:

- a senior management group;
- the participants' immediate manager or team leader;
- the participants; and
- the HR staff.

Developing the Information: The Impact Study

The type of formal evaluation report depends on the extent of detailed information needed for the various target audiences. Brief summaries of results with appropriate charts may be sufficient for some communication efforts. In other situations, particularly with a significant program requiring extensive funding, a detailed evaluation report may be necessary. This report provides the base of information for specific audiences and various media. The report may contain the following sections:

The **executive summary** is a brief overview of the entire report, explaining the basis for the evaluation and the significant conclusions and recommendations. It is designed for individuals who are too busy to read a detailed report. It is usually written last but appears first in the report for easy access.

Background information provides a general description of the HR program. If applicable, the analysis that led to the implementation of the program is summarized, including the events that led to the evaluation. Include other items as necessary to provide a full description of the program.

The **objectives** for both the impact study and the HR program are outlined. Sometimes they are the same, but they may be different. The report details the particular objectives of the study itself so that the reader clearly understands the rationale for the study and how the data are to be used. In addition, this section highlights the specific objectives of the HR program, as these are the objectives from which the different types or levels of data will be collected.

The **evaluation strategy** outlines all of the components that make up the total evaluation process. The specific purposes of evaluation are outlined, and the evaluation design and methodology are explained. Any unusual issues in the evaluation design are discussed. Finally, other useful information related to the design, timing, and execution of the evaluation is included.

The **data collection and analysis** section explains the methods used to collect data. Here, you describe the instruments used in data collection and present them as exhibits. The methods used to analyze data are presented, including methods to isolate the effects of the program and convert data to monetary values.

Program costs are presented in this section, which includes a summary of the costs by category. For example, analysis, development, implementation, and evaluation costs are recommended categories for cost presentation. You should also briefly explain the assumptions made in developing and classifying costs.

The **reaction and satisfaction** section delineates the data you collected from key stakeholders (the participants involved in the process) to measure their reactions to the program and levels of satisfaction with various issues and parts of the process. You may also include other input from the sponsor or managers to show the levels of satisfaction.

The **learning** section consists of a brief summary of the formal and informal methods for measuring learning. It explains how participants have learned new processes, skills, tasks, procedures, and practices.

The **application and implementation** section shows how the program was actually implemented and the success with the application of new skills and knowledge. This section also addresses implementation issues, including any major success and/or lack of success.

Business impact (if applicable) shows the actual business impact measures reflecting the business needs that provided the basis for the program.

Figure 19. Table of Contents for an Impact Study Report

- Executive Summary
- General Information
  — Background
  — Objectives of Study
- Methodology for Impact Study
  — Levels of Evaluation
  — Collecting Data
  — Isolating the Effects of HR
  — Converting Data to Monetary Values
  — Assumptions
- Data Analysis Issues
- Program Costs
- Results: General Information
  — Response Profile
  — Success with Objectives
- Results: Reaction and Satisfaction
  — Data Sources
  — Data Summary
  — Key Issues
- Results: Learning
  — Data Sources
  — Data Summary
  — Key Issues

- Results: Application and Implementation
  — Data Sources
  — Data Summary
  — Key Issues
- Results: Business Impact (optional)
  — General Comments
  — Linkage with Business Measures
  — Key Issues
- Results: ROI and Its Meaning (optional)
- Results: Intangible Measures
- Barriers and Enablers
  — Barriers
  — Enablers
- Conclusions and Recommendations
  — Conclusions
  — Recommendations
- Exhibits

This data summary shows the extent to which business performance has changed because of the program implementation.

Return on investment (if applicable) shows the ROI calculation along with the BCR. It compares the ROI value to what was expected and provides an interpretation of the ROI calculation.

The **intangible measures** section shows the various intangible measures directly linked to the program. Intangibles are those measures purposely not converted to monetary values.

The section on **barriers and enablers** reveals the various problems and obstacles inhibiting the success of the HR program and presents them as barriers to implementation. Also, factors or influences that had a positive effect on the program are included as enablers. Together, they provide insight into what can hinder or enhance programs in the future.

Conclusions and recommendations are based on all the results. If appropriate, present a brief explanation of how each conclusion was reached. You may also provide a list of recommendations or changes in the program, if appropriate, along with a short explanation of each recommendation.

These components make up the major parts of a complete evaluation report. Figure 19 shows the table of contents from a typical evaluation report.

This report is an effective, professional way to present data. You should clearly explain the methodology along with assumptions made in the analysis. The reader should readily see how the data were developed and how the specific steps were followed to make the process more conservative, credible, and accurate. Place detailed statistical analyses in an appendix.

Because this document reports the success of group of employees, complete credit for the success must go to the stakeholders involved. Their performance generated the success. Boasting about results should be avoided. Although the evaluation may be accurate and credible, it still may have some subjective issues.

Selecting Communication Media

Many options are available to communicate program results. In addition to the impact study report, the most frequently used media are meetings, interim and progress reports, the organization's publications, e-mail, brochures, web sites, and case studies. The following sections describe the use of these media for communicating evaluation results.

Meetings

In addition to meetings with the sponsor to discuss results, other meetings are fertile opportunities for communicating program results. All organizations have a variety of meetings where HR results are an important part. For example:

- staff meetings designed to review progress, discuss current problems, and distribute information;
- manager meetings;
- best-practices meetings; and
- business-update meetings to review progress and plans.

You can integrate a few highlights of major program results into these meetings to build interest, commitment, and support for HR initiatives. Along the selected results, you should mention operating issues, plans, and forecasts.

Interim and Progress Reports

Although usually limited to large evaluation projects, a highly visible way to communicate results is through interim and routine memos and reports. Published or disseminated via the intranet on a periodic basis, these reports inform management about the status of the program, to communicate the interim results achieved in the program, and to activate needed changes and improvements. A more subtle reason for the report is to gain additional support and commitment from the management group.

The Organization's Communication Tools

To reach a wide audience, HR staff can use in-house publications. Whether a newsletter, magazine, newspaper, or web site file, these types of media usually reach all employees. The information can be quite effective if communicated appropriately. The scope should be limited to general interest articles, announcements, and interviews.

E-Mail and Web Sites

Internal and external web pages on the Internet, companywide intranets, and e-mail are excellent vehicles for releasing results, promoting ideas, and informing employees and other target groups about HR results. E-mail, in particular, provides a virtually instantaneous means with which to communicate and solicit response from large numbers of people.

Brochures and Pamphlets

A brochure might be appropriate for voluntary HR programs conducted on a continuing basis. A brochure should be attractive, present a complete description of the program, and include a major section devoted to the results achieved. Measurable results and reactions from participants, or even direct quotes from individuals, could add spice to an otherwise dull brochure. Also, the results may provide convincing data that the HR program is successful.

Case Studies

Case studies are an effective way to communicate the results of an HR program. Develop case studies for major evaluation projects. A typical case study describes the situation, provides appropriate background information (including the events that led to the implementation of the program), presents the techniques and strategies used to develop the study, and highlights the key issues in the program. Case studies tell an interesting story of how the evaluation was developed and the problems and concerns identified along the way. Case studies provide a way to document history about the program and its success, to convince prospective sponsors that HR programs add value, and to communicate to external groups about the success with HR.

Communicating the Information

Perhaps the greatest challenge of communication is the actual delivery of the message. This can be accomplished in a variety of ways and settings based on the target audience and the media selected for the message. Three particular approaches deserve additional coverage. Each approach is explored in more detail in the following sections.

Providing Feedback during Program Implementation

One of the most important reasons for collecting reaction, satisfaction, and learning data is to provide feedback quickly so adjustments or changes can be made in the program. In most programs, data are routinely collected and quickly communicated to a variety of groups. Some of these feedback sessions result in identifying specific actions that need to be taken. This process becomes comprehensive and needs to be managed in a proactive way. Table 31 presents the steps for providing feedback and managing the feedback process (Block, 2000).

Following these steps will help move the project forward and provide important feedback, often ensuring that adjustments are supported and made.

Table 31. Steps to Provide Feedback during Program Implementation

Communicate quickly.

Simplify the data.

Examine the role of the HR staff and the program's sponsor in the feedback situation.

Use negative data in a constructive way.

Use positive data in a cautious way.

Choose the language of the meeting and communication very carefully.

Ask the sponsor for reactions to the data.

Ask the sponsor for recommendations.

Use support and confrontation carefully.

React and act on the data.

Secure agreement from all key stakeholders.

Keep the feedback process short.

Presenting Impact Study Data to Senior Management

One of the most challenging and stressful communications is presenting an impact study to the senior management team, a group that usually serves as the sponsor of a program. The challenge is to convince this highly skeptical and critical group that outstanding results have been achieved, if indeed they have. This communication must happen within a reasonable timeframe, address the salient points, and ensure that the managers understand the process.

Two particular issues can create challenges. First, if the results are very impressive, **it may be difficult to achieve buy-in** from the managers who are reluctant to believe the data. On the other extreme, if the data are negative, **it can be a challenge to make sure managers do not overreact to negative results** and look for someone to blame. Table 32 presents guidelines that can help make sure this process is planned and executed properly.

Figure 20 is an example of a one-page summary that could be sent to the management team if they understand the process. Collectively, these steps shown in this example can help you prepare for and present one of the most critical meetings with the management team.

Table 32. Communicating Impact Studies to Senior Management

1. Plan a face-to-face meeting with senior team members for the first one or two major impact studies.
2. When making the initial presentation, postpone distribution of the results until the end of the session.
3. Present the evaluation process, step by step.
4. When presenting the results, reveal the data one level at a time.
5. Show the consequences of obtaining additional accuracy if it is an issue.
6. After a group has had a face-to-face meeting with a couple of presentations, communications may be streamlined.
7. Make adjustments for next communication.

Routine Communication with Executive Management and Sponsors

No group is more important than top executives when it comes to routine communication of HR results. In many situations, this group is also the sponsor. Improving communications with this group requires developing an overall strategy, which may include all or part of the following actions.

- *Strengthen the relationship with executives.* An informal and productive relationship should be established between the HR manager and the top executive at the location where the program is implemented. Each should feel comfortable discussing needs and results. One approach is to establish frequent, informal meetings with the executive to review problems with current projects and discuss other performance problems/opportunities in the organization. Frank and open discussions can provide the executive with insight not possible from any other source.
- *Show how HR programs have helped solve major problems.* Although hard results from recent programs are comforting to an executive, solutions to immediate problems may be more convincing. This is an excellent opportunity to discuss future programs for impact analysis or ROI evaluation.

Figure 20. One-Page Summary of Impact Study[18]

ROI Impact Study

Program Title: Preventing Sexual Harassment

Target Audience: First and Second Level Mgrs (655); Secondary: All employees through group meetings (6,844).

Duration: 1 day, 17 sessions

Technique to Isolate Effects of Program: Trend analysis; participant estimation

Technique to Convert Data to Monetary Value: Historical costs; internal experts

Fully-loaded Program Costs: $277,987

Results

Level 1: Reaction/ Satisfaction	Level 2: Learning	Level 3: Application	Level 4: Impact	Level 5: ROI	Intangible Benefits
93% provided action items	65% increase posttest vs. pretest Skill practice demonstration	96% conducted meetings and completed meeting record 4.1 out of 5.0 on behavior survey 68% report all action items complete 92% report some action items complete	Turnover reduction: $2,840,632 Complaint reduction: $360,276 Total improvement: $3,200,908	1,051%	Job satisfaction Reduced absenteeism Stress reduction Better recruiting

■ *Distribute program results.* When a program has achieved significant results, make appropriate top executives aware of them by providing them with a one-page summary (Figure 20) or a summary outlining what the program was supposed to accomplish, when it was implemented, who was involved, and the results achieved. This summary should be presented in a for-your-information format that consists of facts rather than opinions. A full report or meeting may be presented later. All significant communications on evaluation projects, plans, activities, and results should include the executive group. Routine information on major evaluation projects, as long as it is not boastful, can reinforce credibility and accomplishments.

■ *Ask executives to be involved in a review of HR.* An effective way to enhance commitment from top executives is to ask them to serve on an HR review committee. A review committee provides input and advice to the HR staff on a variety of issues, including needs, problems with existing programs, and evaluation issues.

■ *Use the CEO/CFO's preferred communication methods.* It is very important to speak the same language as the CEO/CFO, using the same channels and methods.

Analyzing Reactions to Communication

The best indicator of how effectively you've communicated the evaluation of an HR program is the level of commitment and support from the management group. The allocation of requested resources and strong commitment from top management are tangible evidence of management's perception of the results of programs. In addition to this top-level reaction, there are a few techniques the HR staff can use to measure the effectiveness of their communication efforts.

Whenever results are communicated, the reaction of the target audiences can be monitored. These reactions may include nonverbal gestures, oral remarks, written comments, or indirect actions that reveal how the communication was received. Usually when you are presenting results in a meeting, you have some indication of how the results were received by the group. During the presentation, the audience may ask questions or challenge some of the information. If you tabulate these challenges and questions, you can use them to figure out the type of information to include in future communications. You should also note and tabulate positive comments about the results whether they are offered formally or informally.

HR staff meetings are an excellent arena for discussing the reaction to the results communication. Comments may come from many sources depending on the particular target audiences. Input from different members of the staff can be summarized to help judge the overall effectiveness of the communication.

When you communicate major program results, you may wish to use a feedback questionnaire for an audience or a sample of an audience. The purpose of this questionnaire is to determine the extent to which the audience understood and believed the information presented. It is only practical to use questionnaires when the effectiveness of the communication has a significant impact on future actions.

The purpose of analyzing reactions is to make adjustments in the communication process—if adjustments are necessary. Although the reactions may involve intuitive assessments, a more sophisticated analysis can provide more accurate information to make these adjustments. The net result should be a more effective communication process.

Using Evaluation Data to Drive Improvement

Evaluation is a process improvement tool. Evaluation data should drive changes to overcome lack of success or provide recommendations to enhance current success. In addition, evaluation data can provide useful information to enhance the image, credibility, and success of HR and provide recognition to all the stakeholders involved. This section explores the strategies for using evaluation data properly and describes how to monitor improvements generated from the evaluation data.

Adjust Program Design

Perhaps one of the most important reasons for evaluation is to make changes in the design of the HR program. This strategy is particularly appropriate in the early stages of the launch of a new HR solution. Reaction and learning data can indicate problems with content, design, and sequencing. This information can be quickly provided to designers to make adjustments as needed. Even follow-up application and impact data may reveal design flaws or situations where design features need to be adjusted to enhance success.

Influence Application and Impact

Sometimes a measurement is taken to reinforce to participants what they should be accomplishing during implementation. In effect, the measurement is actually reminding them of what they should be doing and the success they should be achieving. This use of data is particularly appropriate with follow-up questionnaires provided before the time the questionnaires are due. Participants are made aware of expectations that influence the success of the program. Some HR managers may argue that this use of data is unfairly biasing the evaluation and measurements influence success. However, if the designers are convinced that this measurement is adding value, then it may be helpful to include it every time so that success can be enhanced. It becomes built into the process.

Improve Management Support for HR

Managers at the middle and top levels in the organization often do not support HR for a variety of reasons. The value of HR efforts must be expressed in terms they understand and appreciate. Evaluation data, particularly showing the application, impact, and even ROI, can provide convincing evidence to these managers so they will enhance support for HR in the future. There is little doubt that the most important reason for using evaluation data is to provide it to managers to build support and commitment for HR initiatives. Nevertheless, this approach works only if the data provided are understandable to and valued by managers. The data items they are interested in are typically application, impact, and ROI data.

Improve Satisfaction with Stakeholders

A variety of stakeholders are involved in implementing HR programs. Evaluation data gives stakeholders a sense of the success of the program. In essence, they become more satisfied with a program when they see the value that it is adding. Application and impact data are particularly helpful for these stakeholders so that they can see that their actions are really making a difference in the organization.

Recognize and Reward Stakeholders

The most critical stakeholder in HR is the actual participant who must learn, apply, and achieve results if the HR program is to add value. When this occurs at the rate and amount that is desired, the participants should be recognized for their efforts. When participants excel, in terms of their application and desired impact of HR on the job, they should be rewarded. Evaluation data provides this important clarification of the role of the participant, giving the credit to the group who actually achieved the success—the participants involved in learning and development processes.

Justify or Enhance HR Budget

In today's economic environment, one of the most important reasons for developing evaluation data is to show the value of HR. In tough economic times, the HR staff use evaluation to justify an existing budget or enhance the current budget. This use of data can only be accomplished if the evaluation is pushed to the levels of business impact and ROI. This way, executives approving budgets can clearly see the connection between HR and value added to the organization. In many case situations, the HR staff evaluates significant projects to enhance budgets in times when other budgets are being cut. Conversely, there are many examples where HR budgets are being cut because data are not available to show the actual value of HR.

Reduce Costs

Evaluation data can show efficiencies generated with adjustments in the design, development, and implementation of an HR program. For example, asking participants how the implementation could be successful with an alternative process often provides important insights into ways to save costs. Asking how the particular program could be improved or how success could be enhanced provides useful information for making cost-effective adjustments. In many situations evaluation data are used to drive changes that usually result in conserving budgets or reducing expenditures.

Entice Perspective Participants to Be Involved in the HR Program

When participants have an option of attending, evaluation data can provide a convincing case for their involvement. Evaluation data can show how others have reacted to and used the knowledge and skills from the HR program. In essence, the participants, through evaluation data, show the advantages of being involved in the HR program. You can include this information in brochures, documents, and other promotional materials to show others why they should be involved.

Marketing HR Programs

Closely tied with the previous use of the data is the development of marketing material designed to let others know about the particular program. Included in the marketing material should be evaluation data that show the success of the program. The data add an extra dimension to marketing by enticing individuals to become involved themselves or to send others to the program based on outcomes, not content. You can only develop this type of marketing message if data are collected to show application, impact, and even ROI. In essence, this dimension provides a strategic marketing focus for HR, moving from the position of trying to sell HR to making HR attractive based on its value proposition.

Expand Implementation to Other Areas

One of the most profitable ways to use of evaluation data is to make a convincing case to implement an HR solution in other areas if the same need is there. When a pilot program, offered in one division, is showing substantial contribution and adds tremendous value to the organization, you can make a compelling case to implement it in other areas if a needs assessment or performance analysis has indicated the same need there. Previously, this decision has been made with qualitative data, often based on reaction to the program. Evaluation data showing application, impact, and ROI can provide a more convincing case for this implementation moving to results-based decision making.

Using the Strategies

The uses of evaluation data are limitless, and the options for providing data to various target audience are vast. Table 33 shows all of the uses of data described in this chapter linked to the various levels of evaluation. This matrix can help you understand how valuable evaluation data can be in terms of driving improvement in the organization.

To ensure that data are applied as they were intended, it may be helpful to draft project plans or follow-up actions that can help track improvements that have been made. For example, if evaluation indicated that a redesign of a program is necessary, it may be helpful to have a plan of action to ensure that the redesign actually occurs. In some cases, this type of data should be provided to various stakeholders and sometimes even to participants themselves. They may need to understand that the

Table 33. Matching Strategies to Levels

Strategies for Using Data	Appropriate Level of Data				
	1	2	3	4	5
Adjust Program Design					
Influence Application and Impact					
Improve Management Support for HR					
Improve Satisfaction and Stakeholders					
Recognize and Reward Participants					
Justify or Enhance HR Budget					
Reduce Costs					
Entice Perspective Participants to Be Involved in HR Programs					
Marketing HR Programs					
Expand Implementation to Other Areas					

evaluation is actually serving a purpose. The specific types of follow-up mechanisms may vary, and several options are available. This final step may be the most important part of the process.

Final Thoughts

This chapter presented the final part in the evaluation process—communicating results and driving improvement. If this issue is not taken seriously, the organization will not be able to capitalize on the benefits of HR programs. A full array of possibilities exists to translate the communication into action. You have been equipped with the tools to communicate the results of program evaluation to a variety of audiences, the first step in helping the HR department prove its value on the organization's bottom line.

CHAPTER 9

Taking a Sensible Approach to ROI

The best-designed model or technique is worthless unless it is effectively integrated into the organization. Even a simple, methodical process fails in the best organizations if it is not fully supported by those who should make it work. As you begin to plan for and implement ROI evaluation, you may encounter some resistance to ROI. Fundamentally, resistance to HR evaluation is much the same as resistance to any change process, but you can minimize resistance with careful implementation of a sensible approach to ROI.

The Basis for Resistance

HR staff members and others closely associated with HR programs usually resist ROI because they think the process will require a great deal of their time, which is already in short supply, or because they worry about the consequences of the final outcomes. These two concerns are not groundless. Implementing a comprehensive, high-level evaluation does take time, effort, and leadership. HR staff may already feel overwhelmed and fear having another more thing to do. The fear of poorly designed or implemented programs being "exposed" can cause resistance. Discovering that a particular HR program really did cost too much can be unsettling.

The fundamental basis for resistance, then, is fear or uncertainty. The top 10 resistors to ROI, listed in the context of comments often made by stakeholders involved in evaluation implementation, are listed in the instrument presented as Figure 21. You can use the instrument to assess the current level of resistance.

These issues can lead to resistance to any new evaluation process. The resistance is amplified when the term "ROI" is used. The remainder of

---

Figure 21. What Do You Think about ROI?

Rate the extent to which you agree with the following statements:
   A rating of 1 = Strongly Agree
   A rating of 5 = Strongly Disagree

		Strongly Disagree			Strongly Agree	
		1	2	3	4	5
1.	I do not have time for ROI.	❏	❏	❏	❏	❏
2.	An unsuccessful ROI evaluation will reflect on my performance.	❏	❏	❏	❏	❏
3.	A negative ROI will kill my program.	❏	❏	❏	❏	❏
4.	My budget will not allow for ROI.	❏	❏	❏	❏	❏
5.	ROI evaluation is not part of my job.	❏	❏	❏	❏	❏
6.	I did not have input on this process.	❏	❏	❏	❏	❏
7.	I do not understand ROI.	❏	❏	❏	❏	❏
8.	Our managers will not support ROI.	❏	❏	❏	❏	❏
9.	Data will be misused.	❏	❏	❏	❏	❏
10.	ROI is too objective.	❏	❏	❏	❏	❏

If you scored:
10–25 = You like new challenges and are accepting of change.
21–30 = You go with the flow.
31–40 = You stress out and resist change.
41 and above = You are a strong resistor.

---

this chapter focuses on specific actions that can be taken to reduce these fears, minimize the resistance to ROI, and use ROI in a sensible way.

Fearless Implementation

You can help people overcome their resistance to implementing an ROI evaluation by first recognizing that resistance is inevitable; it is a part of human nature. Regardless of the reason, any type of change causes a flurry of questions, doubts, and fears. At times the reasons behind resistance are legitimate; however, it often exists for the wrong reasons. An initial step in overcoming resistance to ROI is sorting out reasons resistance exists by separating the myths from legitimate concerns. When legitimate barriers to implementation exist, minimizing or removing them altogether is the task.

As with any new process, effective implementation is the key to success. Without it, even the best process can fail. The best implementation occurs when the new technique or tool is integrated into the routine framework. Successful implementation depends on a series of specific steps, which you must develop.

As you conduct additional impact studies, consistency becomes an important consideration. With consistency come accuracy and reliability. Consistency is achieved through clearly defined processes each time evaluation is pursued. Cost control and efficiency are also issues. Implementation tasks must be completed efficiently as well as effectively to keep costs to a minimum and use time efficiently.

Establish Evaluation Targets

Specific targets for evaluation levels and projects are necessary to make progress with measurement and evaluation. Targets enable the HR staff to focus on the improvements needed within specific evaluation categories or levels. When establishing targets, determine the percentage of programs planned for each level of evaluation.

HR programs are varied; the list includes solutions (retention solution), initiatives (health care cost containment), projects (HR web site), special services (wellness/fitness center), administrative activities (tuition refund), functions (leadership development), and routine processes (variable pay). Regardless of the type of HR program, the first step is to assess the present situation as shown in Figure 22. The number of all programs is tabulated along with the corresponding level(s) of evaluation presently conducted for each program. Next, the percent of programs using reaction and satisfaction evaluation is calculated or estimated. The process is repeated for learning, application, impact, and ROI levels of evaluation.

After detailing the current situation, the next step is to determine a realistic target for each level within a specific timeframe. Many organizations set annual targets for change. This process should involve the input of the HR staff to ensure that the targets are realistic and that the staff is committed to the evaluation process and targets. If the HR staff does not

Figure 22. Establishing Evaluation Targets

	Current Situation	Target
Total Number of Programs Offered	_____	_____
Percentage of Programs Using Reaction Data	_____	_____
Percentage of Programs Using Learning Data	_____	_____
Percentage of Programs Evaluated Using Application and Implementation	_____	_____
Percentage of Programs Using Impact or Business Results Data	_____	_____
Percentage of Programs Using ROI data	_____	_____

develop ownership for this process, targets will not be met. The improvement targets must be achievable, while at the same time, challenging and motivating. Table 34 shows the targets established for Wachovia Bank, a large financial services company with hundreds of programs.

Table 34. Evaluation Targets for Wachovia Bank[19]

Level of Evaluation	Percentage of Programs Evaluated at This Level
Level 1—Reaction/Satisfaction	100%
Level 2—Learning	50%
Level 3—Application and Implementation	30%
Level 4—Business Impact	10%
Level 5—ROI	5%

Using Wachovia' example, 100% of the programs are measured at level 1 (reaction/satisfaction), consistent with practices at many other organizations. Only half of the programs are measured at level 2, using a formal method of learning measurement. At this organization, informal learning measurement methods are not counted as a learning measure. The level 2 measure may increase significantly in groups where there is much formal testing or if informal measures (for example, self assessment) are included as a learning measure. Thirty percent of programs are measured at the level of application and implementation. This means that almost one-third of the programs will have some type of follow-up method, at least for a small sample of participants in those programs. Ten percent of the programs are planned for business impact evaluation (level 4) and half of those for ROI (level 5). These percentages are typical and often recommended. There is rarely a need to evaluate more than 5% or 10% of programs at the level of ROI. Sometimes targets are established for gradually increasing evaluation processes—both in terms of numbers of evaluations and evaluation levels—over several years.

Target setting is a critical implementation issue. It should be completed early with the full support of the entire HR staff. Also, when practical and feasible, the targets should have the approval of the key management staff, particularly the senior management team.

Select Programs for Impact and ROI Evaluation

Selecting a program for ROI evaluation is an important issue. Ideally, certain types of programs should be selected for comprehensive, detailed analyses. The typical approach for identifying programs for evaluation is to select those that are expensive, strategic, and highly visible. Figure 23 is a tool you can use to select programs for ROI evaluation. It is based on six criteria often used to select programs for this level of evaluation.

These are only the basic criteria; the list can be extended as necessary to bring the organization's particular issues into focus. Some large organizations with hundreds of programs use as many as 15 criteria. The HR staff rates programs based on these criteria, using a rating scale of 1 through 5. All programs are rated, and the program with the highest score is the best candidate for impact and ROI evaluation.

This process only identifies the best candidates. The actual number evaluated may depend on other factors such as resources and capability. The most important issue is to select HR programs designed to make a difference and represent significant investments. Also, programs that command much attention from management are ideal candidates for high-level evaluation. Almost any senior management group has a perception about the effectiveness of a particular HR program. Some want to know its impact, but others may not be very concerned. Therefore, management interest may drive the selection of many of the impact studies.

Figure 23. Selection Tool for ROI Impact Study[20]

Selecting Program for ROI Evaluation

Criteria	Programs				
	#1	**#2**	**#3**	**#4**	**#5**
1. Lifecycle					
2. Company Objectives					
3. Costs					
4. Audience Size					
5. Visibility					
6. Management Interest					
Total					

Rating Scale

1. Lifecycle	5 = Long lifecycle 1 = Very short lifecycle
2. Company Objectives	5 = Closely related to organizational objectives 1 = Not directly related to organizational objectives
3. Costs	5 = Very expensive 1 = Very inexpensive
4. Audience Size	5 = Very large audience 1 = Very small audience
5. Visibility	5 = High visibility 1 = Low visibility
6. Management Interest	5 = High level of interest in evaluation 1 = Low level of interest in evaluation

The next step is to determine how many impact ROI evaluation projects to undertake initially and in which particular areas. It's a good idea to start with a small number of initial projects, perhaps two or three. The selected programs may represent the functional areas of HR, such as recruiting and staffing, learning and development, compensations, reward systems, employee relations, compliance, and technology. It is important to select a manageable number so the process will be implemented when considering the constraints.

Additional criteria should be considered when selecting initial programs for impact evaluation. For example, the initial program should be as simple as possible. Don't tackle complex programs until skills have been mastered. Also, the initial program should be one that is considered successful now; that is, all the current feedback data suggest that the program is adding significant value. This strategy helps to avoid having a negative ROI study on the first application of ROI analysis. Still another criterion is to select a program that is void of strong political issues or biases. Although such programs can be tackled effectively with the ROI analysis, it may be too much of a challenge for an early application.

Ultimately, the number of programs selected for ROI analysis depends on the resources available to conduct the studies, as well as the internal need for accountability. The percentage of programs evaluated in Table 34 can be accomplished for about 3% to 5% of the total HR budget. The costs of evaluation need not drain the organization's or department's resources.

Involve the HR Staff

One group that often resists implementing a comprehensive measurement and evaluation process is the HR staff who must design, develop, implement, and coordinate HR programs. These staff members often see evaluation as an unnecessary intrusion into their responsibilities, absorbing precious time and stifling their freedom to be creative.

The HR staff should be involved in key decision in the process. Staff input is absolute essential as policy statements are prepared and guidelines are developed. It is difficult for the staff to be critical of something they've been involved with from design to implementation. Using workshops, brainstorming sessions, planning sessions, and taskforces, the staff should be involved in every phase of developing the framework and supporting documents.

The HR staff sometimes resist ROI evaluation because their programs will be fully exposed, placing their reputations on the line. They may have a fear of failure. HR staff members aren't going to be interested in developing a tool that can be used to expose their shortcomings and failures. To overcome this source of resistance, the ROI methodology should clearly be positioned as a tool for process improvement—not a tool to evaluate HR staff performance, at least during its early years of implementation.

The HR staff can often learn more from disappointment than from successes. If the program isn't working, it is best to find out quickly and understand the issues firsthand rather than from others. If a program is ineffective and not producing the desired results, it will eventually be known to clients and the management group, if they are not aware of it already.

A lack of results can cause managers to become less supportive of HR. Dwindling support appears in many forms ranging from budget reductions to refusing to be involved in programs. When the weaknesses of programs are identified and adjustments are made quickly, ineffective programs can be converted into effective programs, and the credibility and respect for the HR function and staff are enhanced.

Share Responsibility

An easy way to make evaluation routine is to have others do it. In some organizations, this may mean sharing the responsibility of various parts of ROI evaluation with a variety of other stakeholders. An important part of that effort is to include evaluation responsibilities in stakeholder involvement. Involve the stakeholders in collecting, analyzing, and communicating data, and reviewing and interpreting conclusions. They will take ownership in evaluation, and the burden will be lightened for staff directly responsible for the evaluation.

Prepare the Staff

To make the transition to higher-level evaluation, it may be necessary to enhance the HR staff's skills in the areas of measurement, evaluation, and ROI so that they can support the methodology. Measurement and evaluation are not always a formal part of preparing to become an HR specialist or manager. Consequently, each staff member may need to learn how the ROI methodology is implemented, step by step.

In addition, staff members must know how to develop plans to collect and analyze data, and interpret results from data analysis. A one- or two-day workshop can help build adequate skills and knowledge to understand the process, appreciate what it can accomplish for the organization, see the necessity for it, and participate in a successful implementation. The important point is that not only is expertise necessary to develop the evaluation policy and practice and implement it, but also to make it a routine part of evaluation.

Prepare the Management Team

Perhaps no group is more important to measurement, evaluation, and ROI efforts than the management team who must allocate resources for HR and support programs. In addition, they often provide input and assistance in the evaluation process. Carefully plan and execute specific actions to prepare the management team and improve the relationship between HR staff and key managers. A productive partnership requires each party to understand the concerns, problems, and opportunities of the other. Developing this type of relationship is a long-term process that must be deliberately planned and initiated by key HR staff members. Sometimes the decision to commit resources and support for HR solutions is based on the effectiveness of this relationship.

Take Shortcuts

One of the most significant barriers to the implementation of the ROI methodology is the potential time and cost involved in implementing the process. Sometimes, the perception of excessive time and cost is only a myth; at other times it is a reality. As discussed earlier, the methodology can be implemented for about 3% to 5% of the HR budget. However, expenses and time requirements can be significant. Cost-savings approaches have commanded much attention recently and represent an important part of the implementation strategy. The following sections offer some cost-savings strategies that can help offset costs of ROI evaluation.

Take Shortcuts at Lower Levels. When resources are a primary concern and shortcuts need to be taken, it is best to take them at lower levels in the evaluation scheme. This is a resource allocation issue. For example, when an impact evaluation (level 4) is conducted, levels 1–3 do not have to be as comprehensive. This shift places most of the emphasis on the highest level of the evaluation.

Fund Measurement and Evaluation with Savings from the Evaluation Methodology. Almost every impact study generates data from which to make improvements. Results at different levels often show how the program can be altered to make it more effective and efficient. Sometimes, the data suggest that the program can be modified, adjusted, or completely redesigned. All of those actions can results in cost savings. In a few cases, the program may have to be eliminated because it is not adding value and adjustments will not necessarily improve it. In this case, a tremendous cost savings is realized as the program is eliminated.

A logical argument can be made to shift a portion of these savings to fund additional measurement and evaluation. Some organizations gradually migrate to the 5% of HR budget target for expenditures for measurement and evaluation by using the savings generated from the use of evaluation. This provides a disciplined and conservative approach to additional funding.

Plan Early and Thoroughly. One of the most critical, cost-saving steps to evaluation is to develop program objectives and plan early for the evaluation. Impact studies are successful because of proper planning. The best way to conserve time and resources is to know what must be done at what time. This prevents unnecessary analysis, data collection at an inappropriate time, and the necessity of reconstructing events and issues because they were not planned in advance.

Integrate Evaluation into the HR Program. To the extent possible, evaluation should be built into the HR program. Data collection tools should be considered part of the HR program. If possible, these tools should be positioned as application tools and not necessarily as evaluation tools. This action enables the participants or others to capture data to understand clearly the success of the program on the job. Part of this issue is to build in expectations for stakeholders to provide the appropriate data.

Provide Participants with a Defined Role. One of the most effective cost savings approaches is to have participants conduct major steps of the process. Participants are the primary source for understanding the degree to which learning is applied and has driven success on the job. The responsibilities for the participants should be expanded from the traditional requirement of involvement in implementing the program. Now they must be asked to show the impact of those programs and provide data about success. Consequently, the participant's role expands from learning and application to measuring the impact and communicating information.

Use Quick Methods. Each step of the ROI methodology has shortcut methods that are quick but credible. For example, in data collection, the simple questionnaire is a shortcut method that can be used to generate powerful and convincing data if administered properly. Other shortcut methods are available for isolating, converting, and reporting data.

Use Sampling. Not all HR programs should require a comprehensive evaluation, nor should all participants necessarily be evaluated in a planned follow-up. Sampling can be used in two ways. First, select only a few HR programs for ROI evaluation using the criteria in Table 23. Next, when a particular HR program is to be evaluated, in most cases, it is necessary to collect data from a sample of participants. This approach keeps costs and time to a minimum.

Use Estimates. Estimates are an important part of the process. They are also the least expensive way to arrive at a number or value. Whether isolating the effects of HR or converting data to monetary value, estimation can be a routine and credible part of the process. The important point is to make sure the estimate is credible and follows systematic, logical, consistent steps. Be sure to address estimation methods and assumptions when communicating results of your evaluation.

Use Internal Resources. An organization does not necessarily have to employ consultants to develop impact studies and address other ROI issues. Internal capability can be developed, eliminating the need to depend on consultants. Several opportunities exist for HR staff to build skills and become certified in ROI evaluation. The resources provided on the companion CD-ROM offer more details on these opportunities. This approach is perhaps one of the most significant cost savers. By using internal resources instead of external consultants, you can save as much as 50% or 60% of the costs of a specific project.

Build on the Work of Others. You don't need to reinvent the wheel. Learn from others and build on their work. There are three primary ways to accomplish this:

1. Use networking opportunities internally, locally, and globally.
2. Read and dissect a published case study. More than 100 cases have been published. (See the resources listed on the CD-ROM and in Appendix B).
3. Locate a similar case study in a database of completed case studies and contact the authors for more information.

These important shortcuts can help ensure that evaluation does not drain budgets and resources unnecessarily. Other shortcuts can be developed, but a word of caution is in order: Shortcuts often compromise the process. When a comprehensive, valid, and reliable study is needed, it will be time consuming and expensive—there's no way around it. The good news is that many shortcuts can be taken to supply the data necessary for the audience and manage the process in an efficient way.

Using Technology

A variety of software tools are available to help organizations develop consistent processes, use standard techniques, and produce consistent reports. Technology is essential for evaluation. Software not only reduces time to conduct an impact study, but it also help develop and report information, often in the form of a scorecard or report generated by the software.

Although several software packages are available, one recommended software package is from KnowledgeAdvisors (www.knowledgeadvisors.com). This software develops reaction, learning, application, impact, and ROI data. It also generates scorecards and reports.

Final Thoughts

In summary, taking a sensible approach to ROI is necessary to make it successful in the organization. ROI will have some resistance and the key to overcoming resistance is to develop a sensible implementation strategy. The actions identified in this chapter will help smooth fears and remove barriers, ensuring opportunity to successfully integrate, and more importantly, sustain ROI as a routine evaluation process.

This book clearly identifies how HR specialists, managers, and executives can show the value of the human resource contribution. When considering the material covered and the progress made, perhaps it is helpful to revisit the challenge facing human resources from two perspectives: reactive and proactive.

First is the reactive approach. Unless HR shows its contribution, it will continue to struggle as a reliable and thriving part of the organization. Budgets will be cut, influence will diminish, and respect will deteriorate. Many executives are now requiring this type of accountability. Sometimes it is necessary to justify the budgets, or particular programs and projects. From a reactive posture, this is absolutely necessary for the continued survival of the function.

On a more positive note, the proactive approach is very powerful. Some HR executives are showing the value of their contribution and changing the mindset of the HR process and function. They are convincing top management that the human resource function can add tremendous value to the organization. The reality is that many human resource programs contribute significantly to the organization; there is just not enough data to convince the decision makers that this is the case. As expected, there are some programs that are not adding value. Because we do not have the convincing data that identifies where they are failing, we are unable to make improvements. The proactive approach positions the HR function as an integral part of the organization. As a respectable and viable function in the organization, it earns a seat at the table for the senior HR executive.

Individuals are drawn to this methodology as a result of both proactive and reactive thinking. Whatever the rationale, the challenge is clear: action is needed now, not later; steps need to be taken to show the contribution; we can no longer say that it cannot be done because it is being done routinely by literally hundreds of organizations. The next step is yours!

ROI Case Studies

This appendix contains a brief listing of case studies for which the ROI methodology described in this book has been applied in a variety of HR settings including compensation, sexual harassment, safety and health, diversity, retention improvement, leadership, development, and a variety of other issues. These ROI case studies are rich in variety and are offered to illustrate the range of applications that have been tackled with this methodology. Additional information and complete copies of the studies are available from the ROI Institute (www.ROIinstitute.net) and on the CD included with this book.

From the beginning of the implementation of ROI methodology, case studies have been an important tool to understand the issues involved in making ROI work in an organization. Although the number of impact studies conducted annually is hard to pinpoint, our best estimate is that approximately 3,000 to 5,000 ROI studies are conducted each year. This estimate is based on the number of people who have participated in an in-depth certification process to develop skills to implement the ROI methodology. In those organizations, the number of annual studies ranges from one to as many as 40 per year.

The CD included with this book describes available books with case studies. We encourage you to seek additional data on these case studies or research the publications listed in the resources.

Table A-1. Sample of Published ROI Studies

HR Program and Organization Type	Key Impact Measures:	ROI	Reference
Performance Management (Restaurant Chain)	A variety of measures, such as productivity, quality, time, costs, turnover, and absenteeism	298%	1
Process Improvement Team (Apple Computer)	Productivity and labor efficiency	182%	1
Skill-Based Pay (Construction Materials Firm)	Labor costs, turnover, absenteeism	805%	2
Sexual Harassment Prevention (Health Care Chain)	Complaints, turnover, absenteeism, job satisfaction	1,052%	2
Safety Incentive Plan (Steel Company)	Accident frequency rate, accident severity	379%	2
Diversity (Nextel Communications)	Retention, employee satisfaction	163%	6
Retention Improvement (Financial Services)	Turnover, staffing levels, employee satisfaction	258%	3
Absenteeism Control/Reduction Program (Major City)	Absenteeism, customer satisfaction	882%	2
Stress Management Program (Electric Utility)	Medical costs, turnover, absenteeism	320%	2
Executive Leadership Development (Financial)	Team projects, individual projects, retention	62%	2
E-Learning (Petroleum)	Sales	206%	2
Internal Graduate Degree Program (Federal Agency)	Retention, individual graduate projects	153%	4
Executive Coaching (Nortel Networks)	Several measures, including productivity, quality, cost control, and product development time	788%	5
Competency Development (Veterans Health Administration)	Time savings, work quality improvement, faster response	159%	4
Machine Operator Training: ROI Forecasting (Valve Company)	Training time, machining scrap, turnover, accidents, maintenance expense	132%	7
Sales Training (Retail Store Chain)	Weekly sales data	118%	1

References for Table A-1

1. Phillips, P.P. (editor), and J.J. Phillips (series editor). 2001. *In Action: Measuring Return on Investment*, volume 3. Alexandria, VA: ASTD.
2. Phillips, J.J., R.D. Stone, and P.P. Phillips. 2001. *The Human Resources Scorecard: Measuring the Return on Investment*. Boston: Butterworth—Heinemann.
3. Phillips, P.P. (editor). 2002. *In Action: Retaining Your Best Employees*. Alexandria, VA: ASTD and the Society for Human Resource Management.
4. Phillips, P.P. (editor), and J.J. Phillips (series editor). 2002. *In Action: Measuring ROI in the Public Sector*. Alexandria, VA: ASTD.
5. Mitch, D.J. (editor), and J.J. Phillips (series editor). 2003. *In Action: Coaching for Extraordinary Results*. Alexandria, VA: ASTD.
6. Schmidt, L. (editor), and J.J. Phillips (series editor). 2003. *In Action: Implementing Training Scorecards*. Alexandria, VA: ASTD.
7. Phillips, J.J. (series editor). 1997. *In Action: Measuring Return on Investment*, 2. Alexandria, VA: ASTD.

Index

References

Anthony, R.N., and J.S. Reece. 1983. *Accounting: Text and Cases,* 7th edition. Homewood, IL: Irwin.

Armstrong, J.S. (editor). *Principles of Forecasting: A Handbook for Researchers and Practitioners,* Boston: Kluwer Academic Publishers, 2001.

Block, P. 2000. *Flawless Consulting,* 2nd edition. San Francisco: Jossey-Bass/Pfeiffer.

Grossman, R.J. 2002, August. "Paying the Price: Events at Rent-A-Center Prove that When Employers Don't Respect HR Today, They'll Pay Tomorrow." *HR Magazine,* 47:28–27.

Horngren, C.T. 1982. *Cost Accounting,* 5th edition. Englewood Cliffs, NJ: Prentice-Hall.

Kirkpatrick, D.L. 1998. *Evaluating Training Programs: The Four Levels,* 2nd edition. San Francisco: Berrett-Koehler.

Phillips, J.J. 1997. *Return on Investment in Training and Performance Improvement Programs,* 1st edition. Houston: Gulf Publishing Company.

Phillips, J.J., and A. Connell. 2003. *Managing Employee Retention.* Boston: Butterworth-Heinemann.

Phillips, J.J., and D. Hill. 2001a. "Preventing Sexual Harassment." In: J.J. Phillips, R.D. Stone, and P.P. Phillips, *The Human Resources Scorecard: Measuring Return on Investment.* Boston: Butterworth-Heinemann.

Phillips, J.J., and D. Hill. 2001b. "Sexual Harassment Prevention." In: J.J. Phillips, editor, *In Action: Measuring Return on Investment,* 2:17–35. Alexandria, VA: ASTD.

Phillips, J.J., and R.D. Stone. 2002. "Absenteeism Reduction Program." *In Action: Measuring ROI in the Public Sector*. Alexandria, VA: ASTD and the Society for Human Resource Development.

Phillips, J.J., R.D. Stone, and P.P. Phillips. 2001. *The Human Resources Scorecard: Measuring the Return on Investment*. Boston: Butterworth-Heinemann.

Phillips, P.P. 2001. "Executive Leadership Development." In: J.J. Phillips, R.D. Stone, and P.P. Phillips. *The Human Resources Scorecard: Measuring the Return on Investment*. Boston: Butterworth-Heinemann.

Phillips, P.P. (editor). 2002. *In Action: Measuring Intellectual Capital*. Alexandria, VA: ASTD.

Phillips, P.P., and H. Burkett, H. 2001, November. "Managing Evaluation Shortcuts," *Info-line*. Alexandria, VA: ASTD.

Phillips, P.P., and J.J. Phillips. 2002a. "Evaluating the Impact of a Graduate Program in a Federal Agency," In: P.P. Phillips, editor, *In Action: Measuring ROI in the Public Sector*. Alexandria, VA: ASTD.

Phillips, P.P., and J.J. Phillips. 2002b. "A Strategic Approach to Retention Improvement." In: P.P. Phillips, editor, *In Action: Retaining Your Best Employees*. Alexandria, VA: ASTD.

Saint-Onge, H. 2002. "Shaping Human Resource Management within the Knowledge-Driven Enterprise." In: D. Bonner, editor, *Leading Knowledge Management and Learning*. Alexandria, VA: ASTD.

U.S. Chamber of Commerce. 2003, January. "Annual Employee Benefits Report." *Nation's Business*.

Acknowledgments and Attributions

The concepts in this book and CD-ROM were developed by the authors over the last 20 years and have appeared in a number of books. The authors have tailored the contents of this book and CD-ROM specifically for the human-resources audience and have drawn on concepts and material published in:

Accountability in Human Resource Management, Jack J. Phillips, (1996), Boston, MA: Elsevier.

Handbook of Training Evaluation and Measurement Methods, 3rd ed., Jack J. Phillips, (1997), Boston, MA: Elsevier.

The Human Resources Scorecard, Jack J. Phillips, Ron D. Stone, and Patricia P. Phillips, (2001), Boston, MA: Elsevier.

In Action: Measuring Return on Investment, vol. 2, Jack J. Phillips, series ed., (1997), Alexandria, VA: ASTD, **www.astd.org**.

Measuring ROI in the Public Sector, Patricia P. Phillips, editor, (2002), Alexandria, VA: ASTD, **www.astd.org**.

Figures and Tables

[1]Adapted from *The Human Resources Scorecard*, Jack J. Phillips, Ron D. Stone, and Patricia P. Phillips, p. 39, (2001), Elsevier.

[2]Adapted from *The Human Resources Scorecard*, Jack J. Phillips, Ron D. Stone, and Patricia P. Phillips, p. 23, (2001), Elsevier.

[3]Reprinted from *The Human Resources Scorecard*, Jack J. Phillips, Ron D. Stone, and Patricia P. Phillips, p. 25, (2001), with permission from Elsevier.

[4]Reprinted from *The Human Resources Scorecard*, Jack J. Phillips, Ron D. Stone, and Patricia P. Phillips, p. 52, (2001), with permission from Elsevier.

[5]Reprinted from *Return on Investment in Training and Performance Improvement Programs*, 2nd ed., Jack J. Phillips, p. 148, (2003), with permission from Elsevier.

[6]Reprinted from *Return on Investment in Training and Performance Improvement Programs*, 2nd ed., Jack J. Phillips, p. 149, (2003), with permission from Elsevier.

[7]Adapted from *In Action: Measuring Return on Investment*, vol. 2, Jack J. Phillips, series ed., p. 21, (1997), ASTD.

[8]Adapted from *In Action: Measuring Return on Investment*, vol. 2, Jack J. Phillips, series ed., p. 25, (1997), ASTD.

[9]Reprinted from *Return on Investment in Training and Performance Improvement Programs*, 2nd ed., Jack J. Phillips, p. 123, (2003), with permission from Elsevier.

[10]Reprinted from *Return on Investment in Training and Performance Improvement Programs*, 2nd ed., Jack J. Phillips, p. 151, (2003), with permission from Elsevier.

[11]Reprinted from *Return on Investment in Training and Performance Improvement Programs*, 2nd ed., Jack J. Phillips, p. 158, (2003), with permission from Elsevier.

[12]Adapted from *The Human Resources Scorecard*, Jack J. Phillips, Ron D. Stone, and Patricia P. Phillips, p. 221, (2001), Elsevier.

[13]Reprinted from *The Human Resources Scorecard*, Jack J. Phillips, Ron D. Stone, and Patricia P. Phillips, p. 468, (2001), with permission from Elsevier.

[14]Adapted from *The Human Resources Scorecard*, Jack J. Phillips, Ron D. Stone, and Patricia P. Phillips, p. 249-250, (2001), Elsevier.

[15]Reprinted from *Return on Investment in Training and Performance Improvement Programs*, 2nd ed., Jack J. Phillips, p. 237, (2003), with permission from Elsevier.

[16]Reprinted from *Return on Investment in Training and Performance Improvement Programs*, 2nd ed., Jack J. Phillips, p. 237, (2003), with permission from Elsevier.

[17]Adapted from *In Action: Measuring Intellectual Capital*, Jack J. Phillips, series ed., Patricia P. Phillips, ed., p. 6, (2002), ASTD.

[18]Reprinted from "Managing Evaluation Shortcuts," *Infoline*, Patricia P. Phillips and Holly Burkett, p. 9, (November 2001), ASTD Press.

[19]Reprinted from *Return on Investment in Training and Performance Improvement Programs*, 2nd ed., Jack J. Phillips, p. 332, (2003), with permission from Elsevier.

[20]Reprinted from "Managing Evaluation Shortcuts," *Infoline*, Patricia P. Phillips and Holly Burkett, p. 12, (November 2001), ASTD Press.

Additional Resources

Many additional resources have been developed to assist with the understanding, utilization, and implementation of the ROI methodology. A listing of a few suggested resources is provided here.

ROI Basics

Phillips, J.J. 2000. *The Consultant's Scorecard: Tracking Results and Bottom-Line Impact of Consulting Projects.* New York: McGraw-Hill.

Phillips, J.J., T.W. Bothell, and G.L. Snead. 2002. *Project Management Scorecard: Measuring the Success of Project Management Solutions.* Boston: Butterworth-Heinemann.

Phillips, P.P., and J.J. Phillips (series editor). 2002. *The Bottom Line on ROI.* Atlanta: Center for Effective Performance.

Implementation

Phillips, P.P., and H. Burkett. In press. *ROI Fieldbook.* Boston: Butterworth-Heinemann.

Phillips, J.J. 1996. *The Accountability in Human Resource Management.* Boston: Butterworth-Heinemann.

Phillips, J.J., and J. Fitz-enz. 1998. *A New Vision for Human Resources: Defining the Human Resources Function by Its Results.* Menlo Park, CA: Crisp Publications.

Phillips, J.J. 2003. *The Handbook of Training Evaluation and Measurement Methods* (4th edition). Boston: Butterworth-Heinemann.

Data Collection

Combs, W.L., and S.V. Falletta. 2000. *The Targeted Evaluation Process: A Performance Consultant's Guide to Asking the Right Questions and Getting the Results You Trust*. Alexandria, VA: ASTD.

Folkman, J. 1998. *Employee Surveys that Make a Difference: Using Customized Feedback Tools to Transform Your Organization*. Provo, UT: Executive Excellence Publishing.

Gubrium, J.F., and J.A. Holstein (editors). 2002. *Handbook of Interview Research: Context and Method*. Thousand Oaks, CA: Sage Publications.

Hayes, B.E. 1998. *Measuring Customer Satisfaction: Survey Design, Use, and Statistical Analysis Methods* (2nd edition). Milwaukee, WI: ASQ Quality Press.

Kraut, Allen I. (editor.). 1996. *Organizational Surveys: Tools for Assessment and Change*. San Francisco: Jossey-Bass.

Morgan, D.L. 1998. *The Focus Group Guidebook*. Thousand Oaks, CA: Sage Publications.

Schwarz, N., and S. Sudman (editor). 1996. *Answering Questions: Methodology for Determining Cognitive and Communicative Processes in Survey Research*. San Francisco: Jossey-Bass.

Shrock, S., and W.C.C. Coscarelli. 2000. *Criterion-Referenced Test Development: Technical and Legal Guidelines for Corporate Training and Certification*, (2nd edition). Washington, D.C.: International Society for Performance Improvement.

Spradley, J.P. 1980. *Participant Observation*. Australia: Wadsworth/ Thomson Learning.

Westgaard, O. 1999. *Tests that Work: Designing and Delivering Fair and Practical Measurement Tools in the Workplace*. San Francisco: Jossey-Bass/Pfeiffer.

Yin, R.K. 1994. *Case Study Research: Design and Methods*. (2nd edition). Thousand Oaks, CA: Sage Publications.

Data Analysis

Phillips, J.J. 2000. *The Consultant's Scorecard: Tracking Results and Bottom-Line Impact of Consulting Projects.* New York: McGraw-Hill.

Intangible Measures

Oxman, J.A. 2002, summer. "The Hidden Leverage of Human Capital," *MIT Sloan Management Review.*

Communicating Results

Bleech, J.M., and D.G. Mutchler. 1995. *Let's Get Results, Not Excuses!* Hollywood, FL: Lifetime Books.

Fuller, J. 1997. *Managing Performance Improvement Projects: Preparing, Planning, and Implementing.* San Francisco: Pfeiffer & Co.

Hale, J. 1998. *The Performance Consultant's Fieldbook: Tools and Techniques for Improving Organizations and People.* San Francisco: Jossey-Bass/Pfeiffer.

Labovitz, G., and V. Rasansky. 1997. *The Power of Alignment: How Great Companies Stay Centered and Accomplish Extraordinary Things.* New York: John Wiley & Sons.

Knox, A.B. 2002. *Evaluation for Continuing Education.* San Francisco: Jossey-Bass.

Langdon, D.G. 1995. *The New Language of Work.* Amherst, MA: HRD Press.

Patton, M.Q. 2002. *Utilization-Focused Evaluation: The New Century Text* (4th Ed). Thousand Oaks, CA: Sage Publications.

Rae, L. 1999. *Using Evaluation in Training and Development,* London, U.K.: Kogan Page.

Russ-Eft, D., and H. Preskill. 2001. *Evaluation in Organizations: A Systematic Approach to Enhancing Learning Performance, and Change.* Cambridge, MA: Perseus Publishing.

Sujansky, J.C. 1991. *The Power of Partnering.* San Diego: Pfeiffer & Co.

Tufte, E.R. 1990. *Envisioning Information*. Cheshire, CT: Graphics Press.

Zelazny, G. 1996. *Say It With Charts: The Executive's Guide to Visual Communication* (3rd edition). New York: McGraw-Hill.

Software

Software has been developed to support the ROI methodology described in this book and is available in two different options. The first option is a complete system of measurement for all the different levels, which cuts across a variety of programs, providing various ways to analyze data at levels 1 through 5. Using a process called Metrics that Matter, this is a comprehensive measurement tool to bring accountability to HR programs.

The other option is a variety of routines and features to develop specific ROI impact studies. This ROI methodology version can also be used for ROI studies as a stand-alone product. Both products are available on a subscription basis. Additional details can be obtained from KnowledgeAdvisors (www.knowledgeadvisors.com).

About the Authors

Jack J. Phillips, Ph.D., a world-renowned expert on accountability, measurement, and evaluation, is chairman of the ROI Institute, a research, consulting, and workshop provider. He provides consulting services for *Fortune 500* companies and organizations in 40 countries. In addition, he conducts workshops for major conference providers throughout the world. Phillips is also the author or editor of more than 40 books—15 about measurement and evaluation—and more than 150 articles.

His expertise in ROI measurement and evaluation is based on more than 27 years of corporate experience in five industries (aerospace, textiles, metals, construction materials, and banking). Phillips has served as training and development manager at two *Fortune 500* firms, senior HR officer for two firms, president of a regional federal savings bank, and management professor at a major state university.

Books most recently written by Phillips include *Managing Employee Retention; Retaining Your Best Employees; Return on Investment in Training and Performance Improvement Projects*, 2nd edition; *The Project Management Scorecard,; How to Measure Training Results; The Human Resources Scorecard: Measuring the Return on Investment*; and *The Consultant's Scorecard.*

Phillips has won awards for his work, research, and publications from the Society for Human Resources Management, ASTD, and other organizations.

Patricia P. Phillips, Ph.D., is president and CEO of the ROI Institute, a leading source of ROI competency building, implementation support, networking, and research. She assists organizations with the implementation of the ROI methodology in countries around the world including South Africa, Singapore, Japan, New Zealand, Australia, Italy, Turkey, France, Germany, Canada, and the United States.

Phillips's academic accomplishments include a doctoral degree in international development and a master's degree of arts in public and private management. She is certified in ROI evaluation and has been awarded the Certified Performance Technologist designation by the International Society for Performance Improvement (ISPI).

Phillips's publications include *The Bottomline on ROI*, which won the 2003 ISPI Award of Excellence; *The Human Resources Scorecard: Measuring Return on Investment*; and several of ASTD's *In Action* casebooks, *Measuring Return on Investment; Measuring ROI in the Public Sector*, and *Retaining Your Best Employees*. She is published in a variety of journals, serves as adjunct faculty teaching evaluation, and speaks on ROI at a variety of conferences.

SPECIAL OFFER

Send for your own ROI Process Model, an indispensable aid to implementing and presenting ROI in your organization.

Jack Phillips is offering an exclusive gift to readers of Proving the Value of HR. This 11" x 25" multi-color foldout shows the ROI methodology flow model and and key issues surrounding the implementation of the ROI methodology. This easy to understand overview of the ROI process has proven invaluable to countless trainers and HR executives and specialists when implementing the ROI methodology. Please return this page or email your information to the address below to receive your free foldout (a $6.00 value). Please check the area(s) of interest in ROI

Please send me the ROI Process model described in the book. I am interested in learning more about the following ROI materials and services:

❑ Workshops and briefing on ROI   ❑ Books and support materials on ROI
❑ Certification in the ROI methodology   ❑ ROI software
❑ ROI Consulting Services   ❑ ROI Network information
❑ ROI Benchmarking   ❑ ROI Research

Name _____

Title _____

Organization _____

Address _____

_____

Phone: _____

E-mail address _____

Functional area of interest:

❑ Human Resources/Human Capital   ❑ Training and Learning   ❑ Quality/Six Sigma
❑ Organizational Development   ❑ Consulting   ❑ Technology
❑ Performance Improvement   ❑ Change   ❑ Other (Please specify)
                                                            _____

Organizational Level ❑ executive ❑ management ❑ consultant
                         ❑ specialist ❑ student ❑ evaluator ❑ researcher

---

Return this form or contact **Jack Phillips**
P.O. Box 380637
Birmingham, AL 35238-0637
Or e-mail information to **jack@roiinstitute.net**
Please allow four to six weeks for delivery

Additional Titles from the Society for Human Resource Managment (SHRM)

Diverse Teams at Work
    By Lee Gardenswartz and Anita Rowe
The Future of Human Resources Management
    Editors David Ulrich, Mike Losey, and Sue Meisinger

The Source Book Kit

Performance Appraisal Source Book
    By Mike Deblieux
HIPAA Privacy Source Book
    By William S. Hubbartt, SPHR, CCP
Hiring Source Book
    By Cathy Fyock, CAP, SPHR
Trainer's Diversity Source Book
    By Jonamay Lambert, M.A. and Selma Myers, M.A.
Employment Termination Source Book
    By Wendy Bliss, J.D., SPHR and Gene T. Thornton, Esq., PHR

Human Resource Essentials:
Your Guide to Starting and Running the HR Function
    By Lin Grensing-Pophal, SPHR
Manager of Choice: 5 Competencies for Cultivating Top Talent
    By Nancy S. Ahlrichs

Managing Employee Retention: A Strategic Accountability Approach
   By Jack J. Phillips, Ph.D. and Adele O. Connell, Ph.D.

Practical HR Series

Legal, Effective References: How to Give and Get Them
   By Wendy Bliss, J.D., SPHR
Investigating Workplace Harassment: How to Be Fair, Thorough, and Legal
   By Amy Oppenheimer, J.D., and Craig Pratt, MSW, SPHR

Responsible Restructuring: Creative and Profitable Alternatives to Layoffs
   By Wayne F. Cascio
Retaining Your Best Employees (In Action Case Studies)
   Series Editor Jack J. Phillips
Solutions for Human Resource Managers
   By the SHRM Information Center Staff
Supervisor's Guide to Labor Relations
   By T.O. Collier, Jr.
Understanding the Federal Wage & Hour Laws: What Employers Must Know about FLSA and its Overtime Regulations
   By Seyfarth Shaw LLP

TO ORDER SHRM BOOKS

SHRM offers a member discount on all books that it publishes or sells. To order this or any other book published by the Society, contact the SHRMStore.®

ONLINE: www.shrm.org/shrmstore
BY PHONE: 800-444-5006 (option #1); or 770-442-8633 (ext. 362); or TDD 703-548-6999
BY FAX: 770-442-9742
BY MAIL: SHRM Distribution Center
            P.O. Box 930132
            Atlanta, GA 31193-0132
            USA

Using the Accompanying CD ROM

The materials on the accompanying CD-ROM are readable on a PC and are in two formats: Portable Document Format (PDF) and Rich Text Format (RTF).

Portable Document Format (PDF) Files

To open the PDF files, all you need is the free Adobe® Reader®. The PDF files on this disc are compatible with Reader versions 5.0.5 and higher. Adobe Reader or the full version of Acrobat is required. You can download the latest version of Adobe Reader for free at **http://www.adobe.com/products/acrobat/readstep2.html**. See "Getting Started," below.

Rich Text Format (RTF) File

The RTF file can be opened in many word-processing programs. You will be given the option to download this file. See "Getting Started," below. NOTE: The RTF file is "read-only." To adapt it for your use, open the file and save it under a different name. You will be able to edit that new file.

Getting Started

To access the files on the CD-ROM, insert the CD-ROM into your compact disk drive. The disk will AutoRun and open a preliminary screen; click "Next" to proceed. You will see an information screen "Using the Accompanying CD-ROM;" click "Next." The disk will give you the option to either open the PDF files or install the RTF file. If you select the PDF files, the disk will either open those files OR will tell you that you need to get Acrobat Reader from Adobe. Follow the directions on your screen.

STOP!

Please read the following before opening the CD-ROM accompanying this book.

By opening the CD-ROM package, you are agreeing to be bound by the following agreement:

Once you open the seal on the software package, this book and the CD-ROM are nonrefundable. (With the seal unbroken, the book and CD-ROM are refundable only under the terms generally allowed by the seller.)

This software product is protected by copyright and all rights are reserved by the ROI Institute and the Society for Human Resource Management (SHRM®) and its licensors. Purchasers of the book may use the materials on the CD-ROM as part of their own work providing that they include the full crediting.

Copying the software to another medium or format for use on a single computer is permitted and therefore does not violate the U.S. Copyright Law. Copying the software for any other purposes is not permitted and is therefore a violation of the U.S. Copyright Law.

This software product is sold as is without warranty of any kind, either express or implied, including but not limited to the implied warranty of merchantability and fitness for a particular purpose. Neither SHRM nor its dealers or distributors assumes any liability for any alleged or actual damages arising from the use of or the inability to use this software. (Some states do not allow the exclusion of implied warranties, so the exclusion may not apply to you if you receive this product in such a state.)